T0350640

Essays in Ethnographic Theory

The ethnographic essay provides a creative form for new work in anthropology. Longer than a journal article, shorter than a conventional monograph, ethnographic essays are experiments in anthropological thought, probing particular cases, topics, or arguments, to propose in-depth but concentrated analyses with unusual insight. In the past these were often published by research institutes or academic departments, but in recent years the style has enjoyed less space than it deserves. HAU Books is pleased to offer room for renewing the essay as an anthropological genre. Our ESSAYS IN ETHNOGRAPHIC THEORY are published as short books, in print and open-access PDF editions.

How Is It Between Us?

HAU
Books

Director
Anne-Christine Taylor

Editorial Collective
Erik Bähre
Deborah Durham
Casey High
Nora Scott
Hylton White

Managing Editor
Jane Sabherwal

HAU Books are published by the
Society for Ethnographic Theory (SET)

www.haubooks.org

How Is It Between Us?

Relational Ethics and Care for the World

Jarrett Zigon

HAU Books
Chicago

Cover design: Daniele Mcucci
Layout design: Deepak Sharma, Prepress Plus
Typesetting: Prepress Plus (www.prepressplus.in)

ISBN: 978-1-914363-05-4 [paperback]
ISBN: 978-1-914363-08-5 [PDF]
LCCN: 2023945213

Hau Books
Chicago Distribution Center
11030 S. Langley Ave.
Chicago, Il 60628
www.haubooks.org

Hau Books publications are printed, marketed, and distributed by The University
of Chicago Press.
www.press.uchicago.edu

Printed in the United States of America on acid-free paper.

For Sylvia and Lucy

Contents

Acknowledgments

All texts are collective efforts even if, in the end, only one name appears on the front cover. This book is no different. I would like to thank the following persons and group for important conversations, comments, debates, feedback, and support over the years. Without them, this book and the thoughts expressed herein would not have been possible: Talal Asad, Joel Robbins, Jason Throop, Cheryl Mattingly, Thomas Schwarz Wentzer, Rasmus Dyring, Sylvia Tidey, Simon Critchley, Chris Hann, Elinor Ochs, Lisa Guenther, Maria Louw, Alessandro Duranti, Lone Grøn, Lotte Meinert, Anne O'Byrne, Ghassan Hage, Patrick Neveling, Jonathan Lear, China Scherz, Megan Raschig, Joshua Burraway, Samuele Collu, Paul Scherz, Aidan Seale-Feldman, Tal Brewer, Luis Felipe Murillo, Charles Mathewes, Samuel Lengen, Christopher Stephan, Devin Flaherty, and Team Phenomenology. I would also like to thank Deborah Durham for her editorial guidance and support.

Parts of this book are significantly revised and expanded versions of articles that appeared in the journals *Journal of the Royal Anthropological Institute* (chapter 1) and *Puncta* (chapter 2).

Preface

Perhaps it is time to admit that today's dominant ethical theories are no longer adequate to the contemporary condition. This should be no surprise. For moments of transformation and interruption—or what I call breakdown—are oftentimes also moments when already existing ethical (as well as political and epistemological) theories are revealed as inadequate to the new conditions of existence brought about through such transformation. Today, we[1] are most certainly living through such a historical moment—from unprecedented global interdependence and mobility to its populist-cum-fascistic response; from the growing technological dominance of everyday life to the rise of data surveillance; from increasing calls for justice heard around the world to the planet

---

1. Throughout the book, I occasionally use the first-person plural *we*. In doing so, I follow the lead of the anthropologist Rebecca Lester (2019: xxviii) when she writes of her choice to use this rhetorical strategy: "I wish to be clear that these rhetorical choices [to use the first-person plural *we*] do not mean that I presume to speak for all people . . . Rather, such choices reflect my knowledge and understandings of [the topics and issues addressed in the book based on twenty-five years of ethnographic research on them]." And yet, as Lester continues, "I remain acutely aware that exceptions, counterexamples, and alternative interpretations may abound." The rhetorical use of the first-person plural is *not* meant to erase differences that I fully understand cannot be erased—indeed, any attempt to do so would run counter to the very ethical theory I am offering in the book. Rather, this rhetorical strategy is offered as an invitation to the reader to settle in for a hundred or so pages and join me within a certain perspective for understanding what might be meant by the word ethics.

itself calling for justice.[2] Increasingly it is clear that ethical theory has proven itself incapable of addressing the breakdowns these transformations have brought about in our political, social, and personal lives.

We need look no further than the "Big Three" ethical theories—virtue, deontological, and consequentialist ethics—to see that times of transformation and breakdown give way to the development of new ethical theories. For each of these developed as a response to such moments in the past. From the upheavals of city-states being enveloped within empires (virtue theory), to the emergence of Newtonian physics and Cartesian rationality (deontology), to the development of industrial capitalism, colonialism, and their consequent bureaucracies (consequentialism), each of the "Big Three" are best understood as having developed in response to and as eventual support for these worldly conditions. We no longer live in those worlds.

Our worlds are much more complex. Oftentimes today making the simplest decision entails sifting through an overabundance of information (some of which may contradict others), at a speed hitherto unprecedented, with persons who may be situated halfway around the world, through the medium of technology, which itself may factor into the decision even if unbeknownst to the humans involved, at a level of uncertainty that is simply beyond ordinary human calculation. Ethics is no longer about being virtuous in the public square, or mobilizing the law of noncontradiction for moral action, or applying some principles that seem to lead to the best outcome. Far from it.

An ethics adequate to the contemporary condition must navigate worlds connected and intertwined so complexly that situatedness is no longer a description of locality. Rather, situatedness must be understood in terms of relations, no matter how dispersed these relations may be. Indeed, ethical theory today must account for and respond to worlds where it is much more likely that we encounter difference than sameness; worlds where such encountered differences include technologies that increasingly replace and often mimic other humans; worlds where truth and decision are replaced by data and algorithms; worlds that are no longer limited to the human but must be capaciously understood to include a range of nonhuman existents—from animals to geological

---

2.   Just a very few examples: B. Alexander 2008; Connolly 2013; Agamben 2015; Scranton 2015; Berardi 2016; O'Neil 2016; Povinelli 2016; Cheney-Lippold 2017; Noble 2018; Benjamin 2019; Zuboff 2019; Chakrabarty 2021; Dyring 2021; P. Scherz 2022, 2016

formations to climate. In complex worlds, ethical theory above all must not offer preestablished principles, laws, or criteria, but rather recognize that to attempt to act ethically is to do so with risk and uncertainty. The traditional ethical theories are simply inadequate to such worldly conditions.

Recognizing this transformation of our worldly conditions and the concomitant breakdown of ethical adequacy, the philosopher Jean-Luc Nancy has called for an ethics of the world.[3] Nancy's notion of world is more capacious than traditional conceptions of world as, for example, a human-centric horizon of meaning. Rather, for Nancy "existence strives toward" and makes a world, and "a world is this: that everything is here and demands to be greeted insofar as it's here."[4] We could call this—following Ian James—a singularly realist and materialist post-phenomenological philosophy of existence that posits existence—all existents—as striving to make a world in common.[5] This is a process that entails a relational ethics that enacts what I call throughout this book attunement and openness.

Such an ethics begins in between. Just as Hannah Arendt's post-foundationalist political theory rejects the Western tradition's assumption that there is something political that belongs to a supposed human essence and argues, instead, that "politics arises *between men*," the chapters in this book argue that we must reject this same tradition's assumption that there is something ethical about the human as such. Rather, if there is one big takeaway from the book it is that *the human* is an-ethical. For, ethics arises *between singular humans*, as well as *between singular humans and other singular nonhuman existents*, and so is quite *outside of the human as such*. Ethics arises in what lies *between* and is *established as relations*.[6] Consequently, the following chapters will make the point in various ways that the most important ethical question we can ask is: how is it between us?

Do we have conceptual resources for articulating such an ethics? The essays that make up this book are a wager that thinking sociocultural

---

3. Nancy 2017: 26, 47.

4. Nancy 2017: 133–34.

5. James 2006: 9, 202.

6. These last several sentences are almost a direct quote from Arendt's essay in *The Promise of Politics*: "politics arises *between men*" (2005: 95) but with the substitution of ethics for politics and, to bring them up to date, replacing man and men with the human and singular humans.

anthropology along with the phenomenological-hermeneutic tradition (broadly understood) offers the best available conceptual resources for articulating this ethical theory. In contrast to, for example, analytic philosophy, which has mostly turned away from the world to focus on such things as mind experiments or strict logical analyses of argument, sociocultural anthropology and the phenomenological-hermeneutic tradition have both—in their own ways—largely focused their inquisitive and theoretical gaze on the lived and experienced messiness of the world. Put another way, these are the best intellectual resources we have for thinking the untidiness of existence and how one, nevertheless, makes their way as a part of it.

Recently, some anthropologists have explicitly engaged other disciplines in their anthropological theorizing to creatively develop concepts in an interdisciplinary manner. Thus, for example, Joel Robbins has written a book of what he calls interdisciplinary anthropological theorizing through a transformative dialogue with theology, Veena Das has done something similar through a deep engagement with the philosophy of Wittgenstein, and Nils Bubandt and Thomas Schwarz Wentzer have edited a collection of essays written by various anthropologists showing "how the encounter between philosophy and fieldwork is fertile ground for analytical insight to emerge."[7] This book is an attempt to contribute to this emerging literature.

Like these recent interdisciplinary engagements, I do not invoke anthropology as a resource for relativized descriptions of local ways of being. In these chapters, I am not particularly interested in describing, as the saying goes, how the natives think or act. I believe anthropology has much more to offer than that. I take it that anthropology has something to say about the very structure of social and human existence.[8] In particular, as a longtime contributor to what is now called the anthropology of ethics, I want to say something about the structure of what has been called moral experience.[9]

---

7.   Robbins 2020; Das 2020; Bubandt and Wentzer 2023, quote from back cover.

8.   Please note that I do not mean "structure" in the sense of any of the various structuralisms. Rather, I mean it in the philosophical anthropological sense of that which makes possible. Thus, for example, the structure of moral experience is that which makes possible the very possibility of morality and ethics.

9.   See, for example, Zigon and Throop 2014.

I will say more about this ethical turn within anthropology in the first chapter. But for now, let me note for those who may not be familiar with the anthropology of ethics that in the mid-2000s it had become clear that a number of anthropologists were interested in addressing what they saw as a lacuna within the anthropological literature—that is, a lack of both an ethnographic and anthropological-theoretical focus on morality and ethics. Although several ethnographies were published in this first wave of the ethical turn, the best of this work—in my view—has not been ethnographically descriptive work on this or that way of being ethical in this or that particular society. Rather, the most significant contributions of the anthropology of ethics have been meta-ethical.[10] Indeed, because of this theoretical focus, many of these anthropologists engage significantly and deeply with philosophical texts and philosophers themselves. In so doing, the very question of what it is to be human has often been implicit—if not entirely explicit—within many of the key texts of the anthropology of ethics.

Similarly, my reading of the anthropological tradition in general is that its most significant contribution has been coming to a broad agreement of what it is to be human in a world with others—or what we can call sociality. To be sure, what I take as a broad agreement is regularly articulated in terms of conceptual disagreement and theoretical turf wars. Still, I will take the risk of claiming that most anthropologists today—despite how they might want to conceive and theorize them—would agree that there is now something like an anthropological consensus around at least three aspects of sociality: relationality, situatedness, and sensibility (by which I mean a bodily-affective-cognitive openness and receptivity).[11]

I have a similar reading of the phenomenological-hermeneutic tradition. This is a less controversial reading than that of anthropology. Few of those who count themselves a part of this tradition would likely disagree that relationality, situatedness, and sensibility have been central to phenomenological hermeneutics from its beginning. Still, although such a

---

10. For example: Robbins 2004; Zigon 2007, 2009a, 2014a; Lambek 2010b; Faubion 2011; Das 2012; Mattingly 2012; Laidlaw 2014; Throop 2014; Zigon and Throop 2014; Keane 2015; Dyring 2018a; Wentzer 2018a.

11. Just a very few examples of many: Hirschkind 2006; Stewart 2007; Robbins 2010; Sahlins 2011a, 2011b; Ingold 2013; Zigon 2015; Holbraad and Pedersen 2017; Mazzarella 2017; Amrute 2019; Lester 2019; Strathern 2020.

claim is relatively uncontroversial, much like within anthropology there are disagreements over how best to conceive and articulate them. For example, while Husserlians may insist on concepts such as intersubjectivity or empathy, Heideggerians likely prefer being-with and Levinasians infinite responsibility or transcendence. And yet, the real differences between these concepts do not take away from the fact that each of them attempts to articulate the experience of worldliness in terms of relationality, situatedness, and sensibility.

The attempt to conceive ethics by thinking anthropology and phenomenological hermeneutics together, then, is to conceive ethics in terms of relationality, situatedness, and sensibility. Importantly, these three should not be considered as distinct qualities or characteristics. Rather, they are best considered as three mutually constituting aspects of worldly existence, for together they constitute the very possibility of being worldly—human or otherwise. For example, because sensibility is the bodily-affective-cognitive openness and receptivity of being-in-the-world, it is essential to what makes an existent both relational and situated. For how could one be relational without already being open and receptive? And situatedness itself is both the condition for and conditioned by the temporal arrival of various existents open and receptive—or perhaps as Nancy might put it, relationally striving—to being in a world together.

To be in a world, then, is to be relational, situated, and sensitive. Ethical theory must be adequate to this ontological fact.[12] For nearly twenty-five years I have been trying to think this adequacy with the help of the various people around the globe with whom I have been doing ethnographic research—from Moscow and St. Petersburg to New York City, from Vancouver to Copenhagen to Denpasar and beyond. That research and subsequent ethnographic writing may have focused on particular topics, such as the ways in which some Muscovites experienced the collapse of the Soviet Union and how those experiences altered their moral ways of being and speaking, or the ways in which drug rehabilitation and therapeutics are best considered in terms of ethical self-work and moral transformation, or the ways in which political activism is best conceived in terms of worldbuilding, that is, as the alteration of the ethical and moral relations that constitute our worlds. Most importantly for this

---

12. Inspired by the work of Levinas, some have already attempted to articulate such a theory. See, for example: Butler 2005; Guenther 2006; Critchley 2007.

book, however, is that all that research allowed me to conceptualize and articulate an ethnographic theory of ethics. By this I mean a theory of ethics that has emerged recursively by putting what I learned from this ethnographic research into a critical conversation with already established ethical theory.[13] I call this ethnographic theory *relational ethics*.

The following chapters attempt to articulate such an ethics. The order in which the essays are presented is significant for understanding the development of this ethnographic theory of ethics and how its various conceptual moves come together. Thus, the first chapter is vital for setting the theoretical scene of precisely what I mean by relationality, attunement, and the between, from which the theoretical and empirical work in the rest of the chapters build. The second chapter further develops this relational basis but now in terms of what I call moral breakdown and thinking. I do this theoretical work through the question of how to live in worlds that are often described today in terms of post-truth. The third chapter builds on all of this to articulate the relationality of moral assemblages, which is a concept that helps us make sense of the often fragmentary and incongruous nature of ethical demands and the possible responses to them in our complex contemporary condition. I do this by considering the very possibility of justice in a world increasingly driven by algorithms and algorithmic judgment.

By the end of the third chapter, the general framework of relational ethics is largely articulated. In the remaining chapters, then, I go on to address some of the most pressing ethical questions of our day in terms of relational ethics. In doing so, I try to offer a more convincing way to take up these problems than that of traditional ethical theory, while also adding some nuance to various aspects of the theoretical work I did in the first three chapters. Thus, the fourth chapter considers the ethical dilemmas raised by the increased datafication of our everyday lives, and the concomitant concern of data extraction. The final chapter is an attempt to think ethics beyond the human to offer a more capacious notion of ethics that would include nonhuman animals, climate, and yes, even rocks.

Therefore, while the ethnographic theory of ethics I articulate here emerged from nearly twenty-five years of ethnographic research, I engage some of that ethnographic material only in the first three chapters. Otherwise, the rest of the chapters engage other anthropological,

---

13. On recursivity and anthropological theorizing, see Holbraad 2012; see also Zigon 2018.

empirical, and philosophical/theoretical sources through the relational ethics framework. Throughout all the chapters, however, I hope to show that relational ethics addresses some of our contemporary ethical problems better than the more traditional and still dominant ethical theories, or what above I called, perhaps a bit too glibly, the "Big Three."

This approach is distinctive within the anthropology of ethics literature, as well as within the discipline of anthropology in general. It is, however, absolutely necessary—vital not only for the importance of anthropology's contribution to ethical theory, but also for anthropology's significance in our contemporary worlds. For it is my contention that if anthropology as a discipline is to have a future in our increasingly complex worlds, anthropologists must become more ambitious in our assertion that what we learn ethnographically can be taken up more abstractly and theoretically—that is, contextually and situationally transferable—to address other topics, concerns, and problems in other localities and times. To my mind, this is what ethnographic theory can and ought to offer. It is what I am offering in this book.

CHAPTER I

How Is It Between Us?

"How is it between us?" is the question I would like to consider as the most fundamental of all ethical questions. I will take this consideration up through an engagement with a debate concerning transcendence and the transcendental that has arisen recently within the anthropology of ethics[1]—though what is at stake within this debate has repercussions for the discipline of anthropology in general; indeed, for any study of social life. Ultimately, this is a debate about relationality and the relational structure of social existence. By entering this debate, I contrast what I call relational ethics with ordinary ethics. In doing so, I hope to show not only that relational ethics is a more convincing anthropological theory of ethics, but also that it offers a conception of relationality, situatedness, and sensibility that is more appropriate for contemporary anthropological concerns in general.

The chapter unfolds in two movements. First, I engage extensively with the transcendence debate, through which I lay out some of the basic theoretical concepts of relational ethics. Here I ask for readers' patience—I promise that the work will pay off as you make your way through the various chapters of the book. For the second movement of the chapter, I offer some examples from a long-term research project of mine to show how the ethnographic theory of relational ethics I begin delineating in this chapter has emerged from my fieldwork.

---

1. Das 2012; Robbins 2016.

Ultimately, I hope to make clear that relational ethics begins with a demand that emerges from a situation within which one finds oneself with others, a demand that pulls one out of oneself to respond in a modality of concern and care for the between, where we dwell together. This response is both an ethical and a political one; it is a response that opens possibilities for being-together-otherwise. Such possibilities, I will argue throughout, can only begin with a relational ethics.

Transcendence and the Transcendental

The issue of transcendence and the transcendental within the anthropology of ethics was first explicitly raised, to the best of my knowledge, by Veena Das. In doing so, Das made a dichotomous distinction between conceptions of the ethical focused on "orienting oneself to transcendental, objectively agreed-upon values" and done in "a domain that is set apart," and an anthropology of ethics conceived as ordinary ethics.[2] In response to this claim, Joel Robbins has asked: "what is the matter with transcendence?" He continues by arguing for the place of religion in the anthropology of ethics and concludes that "the ways ritual allows people to touch transcendent values in their fullest forms ... enables the desirability of single values to gain a hold on people that it can rarely manage to secure in everyday life ... [such that] even in the course of everyday life, some of the desirability of values that is produced in transcendent encounters with them must surely still be felt."[3]

What should be noted here, and where I would raise a concern, is that Robbins seems to accept Das's dichotomy that separates the transcendental as a "domain set apart" from the ordinary by means of, in this case, ritual, but tries to argue for a necessary and significant bridge, as it were, between the two. As such, Robbins's argument might be paraphrased as something like this: Das is right to make a distinction between the transcendental and the ordinary, but she is mistaken in her claim that the transcendental offers little, if anything, to the ethics of the ordinary; for the values fully realized in the separate "domain" of the transcendental offer a significant force for motivating ethical life, and ritual and religion are one of the primary transcendental "domains" where this force is

---

2.   Das 2012: 133–34.
3.   Robbins 2016: 780.

produced. For Robbins, then, the transcendental "domain" remains separated from the ordinary yet remains an important resource for everyday ethical life.

Here it is important to point out that while Robbins seems to consider synonymously the two terms "transcendence" and "transcendental," and thus uses them as merely nominal and adjectival forms, Das, to the best of my knowledge, only uses the word "transcendental." The key lines in Das are the following: "I [that is, Das] will argue for a shift in perspective from thinking of ethics as made up of judgments we arrive at when we stand away from our ordinary practices to that of thinking of the ethical as a dimension of everyday life in which we are not aspiring to escape the ordinary but rather to descend into it as a way of becoming moral subjects . . . not by orienting oneself to transcendental, objectively agreed-upon values but rather through the cultivation of sensibilities *within* the everyday."[4]

On first reading, these lines seem rather straightforward as they appear simply to equate "stand away from," "escape the ordinary," and "transcendental," such that the latter just means something like a dichotomous separation from the ordinary. One might be tempted to ask, however, to where would one escape or step away? Where is the not-ordinary in human life? Robbins, at least for the sake of his argument, is fine accepting religion as a "domain" of the not-ordinary. But I'm too much of an Asadian regarding religion,[5] and a phenomenologist regarding the human condition,[6] to go along with that, and instead must insist that we never escape the ordinary. To put this in phenomenological terms, we are always and never with exception embodied beings in the world.[7] Still, Robbins is most certainly correct to point out that for ordinary ethicists "the explicit, the known and believed, the codified rule, values, and the transcendent"[8] are all markers of the not-ordinary. Here, then, we seem to have quite an unusual position taken by an increasingly

---

4.   Das 2012: 134.

5.   Asad 1993.

6.   For example: Heidegger 1996; Merleau-Ponty 2012.

7.   To be sure, Heidegger was no great fan of everyday life. But he recognized that while it may be possible to inhabit different modalities of the everyday—what has been translated as inauthentic or authentic modalities—it is impossible to escape the everyday. See, for example, Heidegger 1996: 41–42.

8.   Robbins 2016: 770.

dominant theory within anthropology that such occasional human actions as making explicit, pondering knowledge and beliefs, deliberation, and invoking rules and values are *not* part of what we have come to call ordinary social life. We might want to ask, then, what is the ontological assumption that founds such a view?

Let us return once again to those lines by Das, and most particularly the last one which tells us that ordinary ethics does not make ethical judgments "by orienting oneself to transcendental, objectively agreed-upon values but rather through the cultivation of sensibilities *within* the everyday." Setting aside the italicization of "within" that suggests that the "everyday" is some kind of container within which life is lived—a container conception of the world that contrasts sharply with the relational ontology that I am articulating—Das seems to suggest that the transcendental is some kind of Realist Platonic realm, where values such as the Good and the Beautiful sit next to one another like the Father and Son, and this is perhaps what Robbins was responding to. Transcendental reads here not merely as that "domain" separate from the ordinary, but something foundational to the very possibility of ethics.

This is what philosophers call the transcendental argument, which today is most closely associated with Kantianism, and goes something like this: X is the necessary condition for Y, such that X is the transcendental that founds or makes possible Y. And while transcendental arguments most certainly tend to posit objective transcendentals as opposed to any kind of subjectivism, they are not posed as "agreed-upon," as if somehow debated and voted on, even if implicitly so. Rather, transcendentals are *a priori* conditions of possibility. That is, transcendentals are part of an ontological framework—let us say—that provide the foundation or ground or condition of possibility for some particular act or capacity or simply for a way of being.

Now the great unsaid of anthropology is the (primarily) neo-Kantian ontological framework or assumptions or transcendentals—that is to say, the *a priori* ground—upon which the discipline is built, and what I find most interesting about the ordinary ethics approach is how it so clearly discloses these ontological assumptions. Elsewhere, I have argued that ordinary ethics—despite the rhetorical emphasis placed on such things as social action and the ordinary—ultimately assumes that individual human subjects come into any world whatsoever with an *a priori* and normative procedural capacity for acting rightly.[9] For Michael

---

9.   Zigon 2014b: 746–64; 2018.

Lambek this is called acting according to criteria;[10] for Das this is acting according to grammar.[11] Later in this chapter, I will make clear that such transcendentally-founded proceduralism, to use a phrase of the phenomenologist Emmanuel Levinas,[12] reduces the Other to the Same in that acting rightly is merely a matter of procedurally projecting onto and subsuming the Other into a version of oneself.

But for now, let us recall that Robbins reminds us that the Latin root of transcendence/transcendental means to surpass or to go beyond.[13] Ordinary ethicists seem to intend something like this when they dichotomously separate the transcendental from the ordinary. Nevertheless, as I have been trying to argue, their ontological assumption does precisely the opposite work: that is, ontologically the ordinary ethical subject is a self-same proceduralist standing over and against that upon which it works. One might think that this "standing over and against" would allow for a kind of relationality. But at best this could only be a quasi-relationality that Marilyn Strathern has shown many anthropologists tend to articulate, whereby two self-same individuals become connected through some medium that is always already ontologically established.[14] Think here of a line that connects two independent dots, whereby the line moves unidirectionally from one dot to the other. The line in this case is articulated as either criteria or grammar.

In contrast to this approach, perhaps transcendence could be thought in something like the opposite manner of going beyond the ordinary. That is, perhaps transcendence could be conceived as an essential constituent of the ordinary and, therefore, as constitutive not only of the ethical subject but social existence as such. In other words, transcendence could be thought as the being-with—the withness—of sociality that allows for the open space between us where ethical subjects become possible. How might this relational ontology of withness be articulated?

A Relational Ontology of Withness

To begin to answer this question, it is worth briefly considering the etymology of the word ethics. The word ethics has its roots in the ancient

---

10. Lambek 2010a: 1–36.
11. Das 2012, 2015.
12. Levinas 2011.
13. Robbins 2016: 771.
14. Strathern 2020: 170.

Greek word *ēthos*, which is traditionally understood to signify "disposition, character in the sense of psychological configuration, and hence comportment, the way in which one bears oneself."[15] Thus, it has become quite easy to understand *ēthos* as the habituated mind-body-affect totality of the individualized human, standing alone, as it were, in a void without context or connection. But as Claudia Baracchi reminds us, "the semantic range of the term [*ēthos*] exceeds this determination and signals that it must be situated in the broader context of custom, of shared usage, and even understood in the archaic but abiding sense of the accustomed place where the living (animals, plants, or otherwise) find their haunt or abode."[16]

Anthropologists have done important work in showing that ethics is indeed "situated in the broader context of custom [and] shared usage." Importantly, the best of this anthropology of ethics is *not* advocating for a simple cultural or ethical relativism through the empiricist description of how the "natives" behave. Rather, it is better understood as a meta-ethical philosophical anthropology that shows the complexity entailed in the understanding of ethics as temporally and spatially situated *ēthos*. If ethics is understood in terms of disposition, character, and comportment, then the anthropology of ethics has done important work in showing how this manifests differentially and situationally.

To ask, "how is it between us?" is, however, to place emphasis on the most archaic—and today mostly ignored—aspect of *ēthos*. Again, as Baracchi, among others, reminds us, *ēthos* should also be understood in its originary and "abiding sense of the accustomed place where the living (animals, plants, or otherwise) find their haunt or abode."[17] This accustomed place of the human and nonhuman alike is where the living dwell. Rasmus Dyring—a philosopher who has engaged significantly with anthropology—argues that dwelling should not be understood in terms of an existential comfort of ordinary life that is socially and discursively ordered and stable. Rather, dwelling "denotes the peculiar kind of liminal comportment" at the threshold between such existential comfort and that which interrupts the ordinary.[18] This "liminal comportment" is what

---

15. Baracchi 2008: 53.
16. Baracchi 2008: 53.
17. Baracchi 2008: 53. See also Heidegger 2011a; Nancy 2002: 65–85.
18. Dyring 2020: 100.

I have called a moral breakdown,[19] and it is precisely here at this threshold—in what I will call *the between*—that ethics takes place.

If ethics takes place between, then how is this understood ontologically? The relational ontology of Jean-Luc Nancy, which he often articulates in terms of "being-with" or "withness," is helpful here. For as he puts it ever so simply, "existence *is with*: otherwise nothing exists." It is important to emphasize that Nancy's relational ontology encompasses both human and nonhuman existence. Thus, while it is certainly important for thinking the relationality of sociality and ethics, it is meant to describe existence as such. As Nancy puts it: "the ontology of being-with is an ontology of bodies, of every body, whether they be inanimate, animate, sentient, speaking, thinking, having weight, and so on." Or, as he puts it even more clearly: the ontological exposure of withness is shared by "all things, all beings, all entities, everything past and future, alive, dead, inanimate, stones, plants, nails, gods—and 'humans.'"[20]

Thus, in contrast to a bounded and individualized self that must find a way to interact with others by means of some internal force such as "will" or some faculty such as "criteria," which is how the human is conceived in various forms of the dominant Big Three ethical theories, here instead we need to conceive the relational self. To avoid the quasi-relationality that Strathern has convincingly shown is often articulated within anthropology—that is, a relation as the connection of two priorly existing distinct entities[21]—throughout the book I will often use the term *ecstatic* relationality or *ecstatic* relational being. By this I mean to indicate *an ongoing flow of out- and in-pouring relational intertwining*.[22] As such, an ecstatically relational being does *not* exist prior to the intertwining that constitutes it. Rather, what and who one is depends upon *how* one extends both outwardly and inwardly beyond the individualized and localized body in a gesture of transcendence. This ecstatic transcendence will become clearer as this chapter develops.

Despite Strathern's critique of quasi-relationality being commonplace within anthropology, some anthropologists have embraced the radicality of what I am calling ecstatic relationality. Strathern's conception of the dividual is likely one of the most influential. For Strathern the dividual indicates that persons are "constructed as the plural and composite site

19. See, for example, Zigon 2007, 2018.
20. Nancy 2000: 4, 84, 3; italics in original.
21. Strathern 2020: 170.
22. See, for example, Mitchell 2010.

of the relationships that produce them."[23] Similarly, Roy Wagner has written of the fractal person, which "is never a unit standing in relation to an aggregate, or an aggregate standing in relation to a unit, but always an entity with relationships integrally implied."[24]

The anthropologist Tim Ingold, furthermore, describes well how we can imagine this ecstatic relationality extending beyond the person: "We can no longer think of the organism, human or otherwise, as a discrete, bounded entity, set over against an environment. It is rather a locus of growth within a field of relations traced out in flows of materials. As such, it has no 'inside' or 'outside.' It is perhaps better imagined topologically, as a knot or tangle of interwoven lines, each of which reaches onward to where it will tangle with other knots."[25] Although Ingold's excellent description of relational being is here limited to life, the Nancean provocation that I take up, and address explicitly in the final chapter of this collection, extends beyond life to nonlife as well. Thus, every existent is an out/inpouring of relations such that what differentiates one kind—a human, for example—from another—a stone, for example—is precisely the temporally extended trajectories of these ecstatic relationalities and how and with what they become intertwined over time.

Consequently, without hyperbole or metaphor we can say that as a relational being you are the world just as the world is you. As an ecstatically relational being, then, the human, for example, does not have dignity, which conceptually is best understood as a property or quality of an object that renders it a subject. Rather, the relational being—all relational beings—are better understood as a miracle, which conceptually articulates the spontaneously emergent and singular relational out/inpouring of existence. To understand a relational being as a miracle, then, is recognition of the singular ecstatic cluster that emerges into existence, becomes for a time a world along with others, and eventually ceases to exist. Today more than ever we need an ethics that is adequate to this miracle of existence.

Transcendence and Levinas

The work of Levinas is vital for taking the next step in thinking such an ethics. For his focus is precisely on articulating how transcendence

---

23.   Strathern 1988: 13.
24.   Wagner 2001: 163.
25.   Ingold 2013: 10; see also Ingold 2017.

constitutes the ethical subject.[26] In contrast to ordinary ethicists, who posit an *a priori* procedural capacity—criteria or grammar—as constitutive of the individual ethical subject, Levinas argues that the ethical subject is constituted through one's relation with the Other.[27] What does this mean?

Allow me to oversimplify: the Other always exceeds any idea of the Other that "I" may possess—for example, in terms of what and who the Other is, what the Other desires, or even how "I" should act with and toward the Other. Levinas names this excess of the Other infinity. Because "I" and the Other are always intertwined in this infinite relationality, "I" must give myself over, or expose myself to the unknowable and incomprehensible difference that is the Other. Therefore, and in contrast to reducing the Other to comprehensibility through a proceduralist act, "I" have what Levinas calls infinite responsibility to the Other. Perhaps more appropriately rendered, "I" must *respond* to the call or demand of the Other. Below, I will return to this concept of responsivity[28] and show how Levinas considers the *form* of conversation as the structure of this response.

For Levinas, not only the possibility of ethics but the very possibility that "I" *become* an ethical subject begins with the Other. This formal structure of the condition of possibility for ethics and the ethical subject is what Levinas calls transcendence. This notion of transcendence, which is another way of saying the ecstatic relationality of being-with,

26. Levinas 2011. Few anthropologists have seriously taken up the work of Levinas; some who have are: Rapport 2015, 2019; Throop 2010a, 2010b; Wright 2018; Zigon 2018.

27. Note that I capitalize when discussing Levinas's articulation of the Other since this is how he renders it in his writings. When I am not directly speaking of Levinas's work, however, I will not capitalize even though my use of the word "other" will have significant Levinasian resonances.

28. The concept of responsivity is increasingly prominent within a certain phenomenologically inspired anthropology of ethics and philosophical anthropology. See, for example, several contributors to Mattingly et al. 2018. Of particular significance for articulating responsivity, see: Dyring 2018b; Mattingly 2018; Wentzer 2018a; Leistle 2023. Although the concepts of attunement, attuned response, and the like that I articulate in this chapter share much in common with these conceptions of responsivity, there are some significant differences, perhaps the most critical being the centrality of a nominative first-person and humanist perspective often prioritized by these thinkers of responsivity.

does not establish a radical dichotomy between the ordinary and some realm beyond, and it does not necessitate religion or some other sphere of values. Rather, it simply expresses the relational structure of everyday existence. Or, in Levinas's words, the ecstatic relationality of transcendence "delineates the structure of exteriority" and thus "makes possible the pluralism of society."[29]

The ordinariness of this relationality is best revealed in Levinas's insistence that it begins in the bodily materiality of the face of the Other. Confronted by the enigma of the face of the Other, "I" must respond. Although Levinas himself would not put it this way, I consider this ethical response in terms of an attunement that does not end with harmonized equivalence but rather is an ongoing interpretive response to the ever-withdrawing enigma of the Other. *Attunement*, in this sense, is the ongoing attempt to be adequate to the excessive and insurmountable gap between oneself and others, and thus never ends in a harmonized totality. Because this ontological gap between oneself and others can never be filled, attunement attends to it with concern and care.

This conception of attunement and its link with concern and care will become clearer throughout the book as I consider it ethnographically and empirically. For example, shortly I will turn to several ethnographic vignettes to show how attunement is vital for understanding the nonjudgment central to harm reduction practices. In subsequent chapters, I show the import of attunement for thinking about such contemporary ethical challenges as truth, justice, algorithms and data, and climate. What becomes clear is that the ethics the world demands today is precisely one that responds in this situationally interpretive manner that I name attunement.

For now, though, it is important to recognize that when this attunement does not occur in a "smooth" fashion, as it were, an ethical demand is made, and one experiences a moral breakdown. Far from the mischaracterization of rupturing the everyday made by those who have critiqued this concept,[30] the experience of a moral breakdown is, in fact, a more intensely felt and considered relational intertwining. Relationality is more intensely felt and considered in the moment of breakdown precisely because the demand[31] of the situation has explicitly called one

---

29.   Levinas 2011: 304–305, 291.

30.   For example: Laidlaw 2014: 117; Das 2015: 106.

31.   In my original articulation of moral breakdown in a 2007 article I adapted and developed this notion of ethical demand from the work of both Knud Ejler Løgstrup (1997) and Simon Critchley (2007).

to ethically attune more attentively.[32] Again, this will become clearer throughout the book in the various cases I offer. For example, I will show in this chapter how in harm reduction contexts such as syringe exchange, ethical demands are regularly placed on practitioners to attune to the specific circumstances of a particular drug user's life rather than following the rules of the exchange center. Or in the next chapter, I show how a Russian woman, with whom I did an ethnographic life history, once experienced a moral breakdown on a train and how this experience pulled her relationally even tighter to her world in the modes of care and attention. Or in the final chapter, I show how feelings of despair felt by many of us about the looming climate crisis are best understood as experiences of moral breakdown that have the potential to motivate us to creatively reimagine our relations with the nonhuman in more ethical and caring ways. The point to be made, then, is that the moment of moral breakdown is that ethical moment when one experiences most intensely the demand to care and attend to the constitutive relational intertwining that gives way to us.[33]

Despite the significance of this relational or transcendent structure for ethics and sociality, the one-sided asymmetry that Levinas posits for this transcendence falls short of the kind of mutuality of being anthropologists might prefer to consider. If for Levinas the Other is separated from me by what he calls an infinite curvature of intersubjectivity, then a task for anthropologists might be to conceive of this asymmetrical relation in more mutual terms without reducing it to a totalized harmonious equivalence.[34] That is, the question might be posed as this: how to maintain the enigma of the Other and the asymmetrical relation this entails, while at the same time recognizing that the Other must also relate to me as an enigmatic Other by way of an asymmetrical relation?[35] In the rest

---

32. Zigon 2014a, 2018. For other anthropologists who have also written on ethical attunement, see: Throop 2008, 2018; Mckay 2018; Amrute 2019.

33. Similarly, Dyring writes of the ethical demand as existential transcendence. See Dyring 2018a: 233.

34. Derrida already raised this question of the mutual asymmetry between the Same and Other in Levinas in his important review of *Totality and Infinity* soon after the latter's publication. To the best of my knowledge, Derrida did not follow up on this. See Derrida 1978.

35. Merav Shohet's notion of asymmetrical reciprocity begins to respond to this question, but ultimately cannot because it does not maintain the enigmatic nature of the Other. For example, one of Shohet's primary examples

of this chapter, I will move beyond this Levinasian incitation and begin to address these questions by turning to what I call *between*.

Between

I have been considering the question of "How is it between us?" as the most fundamental of all ethical questions. Such a seemingly simple question is immediately differentiable from more commonly asked ethical questions such as—"what is the good?"—or—"did she act rightly?"—and in this differentiation its radicality is revealed. When we ask "what is the good?" or "did she act rightly?" there is an assumption built into these questions that there is "the good," the whatness of which we can query, or an exact rightness that can precisely modify a particular act. These questions assume the prior existence of "the good" or "the right" already there as the object or the measure in reference to which the questions could be answered definitively. In contrast to asking the transcendental question indicated by the "what" or "did," a question that begins with the assumption that ethics is an accomplishment of a telos or acting according to a predefined measure, to ask "how" is to ask about an ongoing existential process immanent to situations within which we find ourselves ecstatically intertwined. To ask "how" is to understand ethics as ongoing attunement.

Who attunes? Us. In contrast to the individual who aims for "the good" or attempts to act "rightly," the "us" that attunes is a noncategorizable plurality of singular beings that are neither individuals nor merely part of a collective, but unique instances of being-relational. Thus, the dative first-person plural "us" only emerges as a response to the between of a singular situation.[36] Notice that in contrast to the one-sided, asymmetrical, infinite responsibility to the Other posited by Levinas that I critically noted at the end of the last section, the attuned response of which I write here is *to the between of the situation*. That is, this being-relational

---

is that of filial piety, which if nothing else is a set of asymmetrical relations within which each person knows precisely where they stand in relation to the other. Put another way, there is nothing enigmatic about one's moral obligations to a father, for example, within the relationality of filial piety. See Shohet 2021.

36. For the importance of the dative for thinking the emergence of an (ethical) "subject," see Marion 2002; Wentzer 2018b.

of "us" manifests as an attuned response to this situation now, a situation always constituted partly by others, even if in their absence.

How is it between us? This ongoing attunement immanent to worlds and situations is indicative of the ecstatic relationality that gives way to us. The spacing of this giving way—the place of ethics as *ēthos*—I name *between* but do so with the caveat that this "between" that is relationality neither can be objectified—thing-like—nor contained through this nomination. And yet, this "between" of relationality emerges.[37] How? Phenomenological analysis would disclose multiple responses to this question—for example, through moods or, as I will take up in the following chapter, thinking—but given the limitations of this essay, as well as the regular reference to ordinary language philosophy and Wittgenstein within ordinary ethics, I will focus on one possible response, and that is, language.

Lambek has described how insights from ordinary language philosophy have influenced his rendering of ordinary ethics in the following way: he

> find[s] the wellsprings of ethical insight deeply embedded in the categories and functions of language and ways of speaking, in the commonsense ways we distinguish among various kinds of actors or characters, kinds of acts and manners of acting; in specific nouns and adjectives, verbs and adverbs, or adverbial phrases, respectively; thus, in the shared criteria we use to make ourselves intelligible to one another, in "what we say when."[38]

Similarly, Veena Das regularly invokes Wittgenstein's notion of grammar as central to her version of ordinary ethics, and defines it as "the way criteria tell us what an object or emotion or rule is within a form of life."[39]

A phenomenological conception of language can be contrasted with the *a priori* (articulated in terms of criteria and grammar) of this "ordinary" view of language. A good starting point for understanding an important version of the phenomenology of language is Martin Heidegger's claim that "language is the house of being." What could such an enigmatic phrase mean? When he wrote this in his "Letter on Humanism,"

---

37. See also Crapanzano 2004.
38. Lambek 2010a: 2.
39. Das 2015: 71n.

he immediately followed it with: "In its home man dwells."[40] Humans dwell in language and do so as existing. For Heidegger, as it is for much of the phenomenological tradition, to exist is to be ecstatic—always to be excessively outside oneself intertwined with other ecstatic beings, human and nonhuman alike. For humans, language is one of the primary entanglements of this ecstatic relationality. Thus, it is to a great extent through language that humans are pulled beyond themselves to dwell in between with others.

Notice, this phenomenon is a pulling and not a projecting. Unlike the ordinary ethicists, who begin with a view of language grounded in a prior and already established set of criteria or grammar that is projected out from the individual speaker, a phenomenological view of language sees language as a primary *affective force* emanating from between us that pulls and places demands on us to respond. The manifold responses, which manifest more as listening than speaking, enliven the between by means of their distinction. Thus, the distinctive and manifold responses to the call of language give way to a between characterized above all by difference. A difference, that is, to which attunement is situationally ongoing. This is simply another way of describing ethics.

Heidegger contrasted this phenomenological view of language with more common conceptions of language, which, as he put it, is the notion that "language is the expression, produced by [humans], of their feelings and the world view that guides them."[41] This is the notion that assumes not only that language is structured by a set of shared criteria and grammar, but also can express a shared meaning. Elsewhere, I have argued against the anthropological focus on shared meaning and have tried to make the case that at least in ethical encounters—although I would presume this is indeed the case with most if not all encounters—language does not express shared meaning but rather acts as a "bridge of being" that allows us to be with one another without the expectation of sharedness.[42] That is to say, ethics as ongoing attunement is not about adhering to a preestablished grammar or criteria, and neither is it about finding the slot of shared meaning. Rather, to the extent that language is a modality of ethical attunement, it is that call, that demand, that pull, that allows the possibility to dwell once again with others in the world

---

40. Heidegger 2011a: 147.
41. Heidegger 1975a: 196.
42. Zigon 2012: 204–20.

between us. Language as a modality of ethics, then, calls us—places a demand on us—to be with others in the world in an attuned manner.

Levinas wrote of this phenomenon as conversation. For Levinas, language *is* the relation between the Same and the Other, which is just a fancy philosophical way of saying me and you, whoever the "me" and the "you" might be.[43] Ethically, this relation takes the *form* of conversation. Here it is important to emphasize that Levinas is not arguing that the actual act of conversation is ethics—though at times it may be—but rather that the *form* of conversation can be understood as the formal structure of ethics.

In conversation, Levinas writes, we become astonished. Through conversation the Other is revealed in her strangeness to me. I can never know prior to the Other speaking what she will say, and as such I must listen, and then respond. But I cannot respond with a projection; my response cannot be a claim of "knowing" the Other, and neither can it be a taking over of the conversational relation with the claim that "the same thing happened to me." Because the "same thing" never happens, such a claim is not a continuance of open conversation but rather shuts it down through the colonization of the Other by me. In conversation the Other is revealed as *not* the Same, which means that she cannot be thematized through a projection of an *a priori* criteria or grammar, or the claim of a "shared experience." Rather, to be in conversation is to let the Other be and attune.

It is important here to contrast this letting be of ethical attunement as revealed in the formal structure of conversation with Das's articulation of how the strangeness of the other is confronted in her version of ordinary ethics. Das writes: "could one take away this feeling of something being completely alien to us by imagining the possibility that these connect with things we do habitually?" She continues, "thus enable[ing] us to see the connections between us and an 'other' however far we might be in terms of social conventions because a space of possibility has been prepared through which *we can project* bits and pieces of *our* life to include some aspects of the life of the other."[44] In other words, by means of a projection of one's own grammar, which, again, is defined as "the way criteria tell us what an object or emotion or rule is within a form of life,"[45] the strangeness, alterity, and difference of the other is translated

---

43.   Levinas 2011: 39.

44.   Das 2015: 75; italics added.

45.   Das 2015: 71n.

and understood in terms of the projected criteria for one's own form of life.

Undoubtedly, Das means this in the best possible manner. For she is quite clear that such projecting is part of a process for opening a space of possibility for including the other. Note, however, that this inclusion is accomplished by means of a kind of translation of the other's strangeness into the familiarity of my own form of life. Setting aside the question of whether the other wants to be included in my form of life, Talal Asad is surely right when he argues that translation is accomplished through the dominance of what he called a strong language over that of the weak.[46] Such a translational projection is what Levinas called thematizing the Other, an act he described as one of violence.[47] To be sure, I am certain that Das does not intend this ordinary ethical projection in such a manner, and I am not suggesting it here. But an author's intentions do not always match a work's entailments.

What we see here, then, is the clear difference between two distinctive approaches within the anthropology of ethics. An ordinary ethics that encounters the alterity of the other with a projected attempt to render the other the Same, no matter how good the intentions. And a relational ethics that encounters the alterity of the other through attuned letting-be, thus preserving the between of difference.[48] If, as Elinor Ochs has written, ordinary enactments of language are modes of experiencing the world, this can only be so because worlds and situations are already partly constituted through language.[49] Constituted not, as I have been trying to argue, as worlds and situations of a projected shared meaning or a shared form of life, but rather as the between that pulls us together in our differences in the modalities of concern and care.

This concern and care are indicative of ethical attunement. To understand this, we need to make an important distinction between translation and interpretation. If translation, as Asad argues, is a matter of the dominant projection of the Same onto the other, then interpretation is the ongoing attunement of being-with-understandably at this moment now.[50] Ethical attunement as interpretation, then, does not result in the harmonization of equivalence, and neither does it end in a fusion of

---

46. Asad 1986.
47. For example, Levinas 2011: 43, 65, 70 and 291. See also Butler 2005.
48. See also Zigon 2019.
49. Ochs 2012.
50. Caputo 2018: 139.

horizons.[51] Rather, ethical attunement as interpretation does not end; it is above all the ongoing risk of responding situationally to the astonishment evoked by the unknowability of the other to whom one is exposed. Importantly, then, ethics cannot be measured or judged by its return to the *a priori* of "the good" or "the right." Ethics cannot be reduced to repetition. Rather, ethics must be conceived as the movement toward an otherwise.

How is it between us? This is the most fundamental of all ethical questions because as humans we can only live together in worlds and situations as intertwined in a between that is all we can ever share. It is for this reason that Hannah Arendt argued that we are concerned and care for the between because we have an interest in its being, for the between is essential to the human condition.[52] We are concerned and care in our interest—in our *inter-est*—that is, in our being-between as being-relational. For Arendt, this entailed not only ethical activity but also political activity. In this sense, if "how is it between us?" is the most fundamental of all ethical questions, then it is fundamentally a political question as well.

Harm Reduction as Relational Ethics and Politics

So far, I have been working at a rather abstract and theoretical level. This has been important and necessary work for setting the theoretical scene for what comes in the rest of this book. But now I'd like to turn to a brief example or two from one of my ethnographic projects. In doing so, I hope to show how the ethnographic theory of ethics—relational ethics—that I have started to delineate in this chapter has emerged out of my ethnographic research. The result is an anthropologically grounded theory of ethics that in some of the subsequent chapters of this book I take up in contexts beyond my ethnographic work to address some of today's most pressing ethical concerns. This will be important for showing that ethnographic theory can be utilized in other contexts such that anthropology can have impact beyond the particularity of fieldwork. But I don't want to get ahead of myself. For now, I want simply and briefly to show how relational ethics first emerged from my ethnographic research,

---

51. Cf. Gadamer 1997.
52. Arendt 1998.

and here I will focus on my fieldwork with harm reduction practitioners and anti-drug war activism.

In the early 2000s, I began doing anthropological research on the therapeutic, public health, ethical, and political responses to drug use and the war on people who use drugs (more commonly known as the war on drugs). This research was done in various places across the globe—from Russia to the United States, from Canada to Indonesia to Denmark.[53] In contrast to more traditional multisited research, I did what I call an assemblic ethnography, which is a method of chasing and tracing a complex phenomenon (the war on drugs) through its continual process of assembling across different global scales and its temporally differential localization.[54] For example, in 2006 I began research at a Russian Orthodox-run rehabilitation program in Russia, during which I became aware of the political struggle there for harm reduction services. This led me to the central role of user unions in this struggle, which had been initially funded by the Open Society Foundation based in New York. While in New York researching this initiative, I learned about VOCAL-NY,[55] a local political organization dedicated to fighting the drug war and its pernicious consequences, and how they politically address their drug war situation, which, I came to learn, was partly informed by the successes in Vancouver, where I then went, and so on to Copenhagen, Denpasar, and elsewhere.

Importantly, my research did not simply move from one site to the next, but rather *moved along diverse assemblic relations* of the drug war. The example I just provided thus describes my movement along the biopolitical therapeutic relational aspect of the drug war as I traced it from Russia to New York to Vancouver to Copenhagen and beyond. Another example would be my tracing of the carceral political-economics and state-based surveillance relational aspect of the drug war from, for example, New York to Denpasar and back again to Russia. In contrast to a project with one or several fieldwork sites, then, this research unfolded along assemblic relations as they become differentially distributed globally.

The relational ethics I am articulating in these chapters partially emerged from this ethnographic archive. To illustrate this, I draw from

---

53. For example, Zigon 2011, 2019.
54. Zigon 2015, 2018, 2019.
55. VOCAL-NY is the organization's actual name, and it is used with permission.

18

my time in New York City and Vancouver in the early and mid-2010s (though very similar things could be said about harm reduction practices I've observed and taken part in at other locations and times). In doing so, I show how relational ethics as illustrated in the "philosophy" and practice of harm reduction demands that one attunes to the between. In this way, the practice of harm reduction in the very process of carrying out its pragmatic mandate of, for example, preventing overdose or the spread of infectious disease, also opens possibilities for dwelling together. What I hope to show with these ethnographic examples, then, is how a relational ethics not only responds to the enigmatic alterity of an other with an attuned care that respectfully preserves the other's singularity, but at the very same time attends to the between as a site of potentiality for being-together-with-one-another.

Harm reduction is an approach to drug use that begins with a very simple premise: people use drugs, in most cases they will continue to do so until they "choose" no longer to do so, and in the meantime conditions should be such as to reduce as much as possible the potential harm (e.g., overdose and the spread of infectious disease) drug use can have on both users and non-users alike. While syringe exchange is likely the best-known harm reduction practice, there are others that are just as significant even if less prevalent. For example, clean "works" (e.g., cotton, water, tourniquets, alcohol swabs, and Band-Aids), as far as I know, are always distributed along with syringes; condoms regularly are as well. Substitution therapy (e.g., methadone and buprenorphine) is also a common harm reduction practice, but less so than syringe and "works" distribution. Even less common are supervised consumption sites, where people can use drugs with a trained "supervisor" nearby. And even less common is heroin prescription, which allows users to get heroin without worry of such things as police harassment, the purchase of contaminated drugs, and violence in the context of purchasing from a dealer. Heroin prescription is also regularly connected with supervised consumption sites and the provisioning of clean syringes and works, and as such is likely the best example of what harm reduction can be.

There is no doubt that in many places harm reduction has become intertwined with the biopolitical therapeutic aspect of the drug war, and thus its implementation has resulted in the increased institutionalization of harm reduction, along with the consequent disciplinary effects of shaping specific kinds of persons. Much has been written on this.[56]

---

56.   For example: Bourgois 2000; Roe 2005; K. McLean 2011; Zigon 2011.

In this section, however, I will focus on the essential "principle" of harm reduction, i.e., nonjudgment, and how it illustrates well a relational ethics concerned above all with how it is between us. This is so because nonjudgment goes beyond the withholding of judgment, and therefore beyond the projection of a preestablished criteria onto an other, and instead entails the freeing up of a site of potentiality—a between—for an otherwise modality of being-with to emerge.

Nonjudgment is essential to harm reduction because unlike all other ways of addressing drug use today, harm reduction does not begin from the perspective that drug use is bad or evil and must be stopped. Harm reduction does not project a judgment upon the other based on preestablished criteria for evaluating drug use. Rather, harm reduction begins with the acceptance that drug use occurs and will continue to occur. Consequently, worlds must be built and a between must be maintained such that the possible dangers of drug use—note, by this is not meant the evils—are minimized. Harm reduction begins with no judgment about drug use or drug users other than that it and they exist.

This, of course, does not mean that everyone who practices harm reduction supports drug use. Many, in fact, do not. Indeed, every harm reductionist I have ever spoken with is fully aware of the possible health, social, and personal dangers of drug use. Nonjudgment, then, does not mean full-on support of drug use. Rather, I would like to make the case that nonjudgment, as the essence of harm reduction, is what I am trying to describe in these chapters as the ethical (and political) response made to the demand of the situation called the drug war; a response not of projecting already established criteria, but rather a giving way to the pull of the between that calls for attuned care and concern.

For to be a harm reductionist entails that one does not exert their sovereign will on others and their worlds by projecting and imposing certain criteria of how or what should be. Rather, to be a harm reductionist is to accept that drug use happens, and to listen and respond to the singularity of the drug user(s) whom one is with. In so doing, harm reductionists both ethically attend to the between such that new possibilities emerge for users and non-users to live together, and politically attempt to build a world in which drug use does not result in the dehumanization, ill health, or death of users and non-users alike.

In other words, to practice harm reduction is to let-users-be, attune, and to build worlds that are open to this letting-be. While politically this entails processes of worldbuilding, ethically this entails a concern for the between where we dwell together with others in potentiality. Here we can see how attuned letting-be is not a fatalistic stance of nonparticipation. Rather, it is an ethical modality of intense relationality that is concerned and cares for the between oneself and others. This relational ethics, furthermore, has the political consequence of transforming worlds to become places characterized above all by letting-be and attunement.

At its most foundational point, the relational ethics and politics enacted through harm reduction begin with the syringe exchange program. This program provides the opportunity for drug users to bring used syringes to the exchange to receive clean and unused syringes in return, along with other necessary "works" such as cotton, sterile water, and bottle caps. In most cases the exchange is one for one, such that if, for example, someone brings in twenty used syringes, they can receive twenty new ones in return. In some locations, such as the exchange where I worked in New York (although I suspect this is true nearly everywhere, as I've witnessed it in a number of other places), there is some leeway in this rule such that if a sufficient reason is given for why a person needs more syringes than he brought in, he is able to receive a certain number more. Although what counts as a sufficient reason is already institutionally predefined, I have found that in practice the harm reductionist on duty accepts almost any reason given.

This is a key observation for it indicates that despite the institutional context predefined by certain criteria of interaction, a relational ethics overrides, as it were, the criteria such that the harm reductionist responds to the ethical demand of the situation she finds herself in with this particular drug user now. The ethical demand in this case is not simply a request made by the drug user for more syringes than the rule allows. Rather, the demand is to attune to the situation that has emerged between oneself and the singularity of this particular drug user, and why adhering to criteria in this instance may be more harmful than not. Oftentimes, a drug user makes such a request because following the rule would foreclose other possibilities in their life, such as traveling to visit a family member, or being able to take a new job with hours that conflict with those of the harm reduction center. Such requests of exceptions to the rule evoke an ethical demand on the harm reductionist to attune to the singularity of the user, the particularity of this situation now, and the possibilities that would become available by means of such attunement.

It is also an ethical demand that the harm reductionist become concerned for the between mutually inhabited by them and others; a concern that pulls the harm reductionist beyond herself and the institutional criteria she is charged to implement in the recognition that she and the drug user are at that moment mutually caring for the between themselves and all potential others. It is important to emphasize that "all potential others" are indeed constitutive of the between at issue here. For one of the fundamental aims of syringe exchange is the prevention of the spread of infectious diseases to others beyond this particular drug user here right now. In this very simple and routine syringe exchange interaction, then, we see how becoming concerned with how it is between us begins with the nonjudgment of letting the other be, and how this letting-be allows one to be pulled beyond oneself in response to the ethical demand that emerges in the situation at hand. A response, that is, that is not the mere application of a rule or criteria.

In most places around the globe such interactions that enact this relational ethics of harm reduction are limited primarily to rather isolated centers where a few services such as syringe exchange are provided. But as I show in *A War on People*,[57] the Downtown Eastside of Vancouver, to the best of my knowledge, is the only place where harm reduction has become a dispersed aspect of the ordinary life of that world, such that it is now impossible to be farther than just a few minutes from some form of harm reduction in the neighborhood. As a result, the relational ethics and its concomitant political activity practiced in the Downtown Eastside (DTES) has become an exemplar for many within the global anti-drug war movement, which in its activity against the war on drugs ends up having social and political effects that go well beyond a singular focus on the illegality of drugs. In the third chapter of the book, I consider this movement in much detail.

What tends to get the most attention in the DTES is the fact that a coalition of drug users, harm reductionists, and allied organizations were able to establish the first legally sanctioned safe injection site (Insite) in North America, which has become the central core from which the ordinariness of harm reduction radiates. Although the establishment of Insite is certainly a great accomplishment and a central aspect of the new world that has emerged there, it is just one aspect of this new world of the DTES. Redesigned as a world of nonjudgment, where drug users are let be to dwell, the DTES now consists of, among other things, art galleries and studios, a bank, a grocery store, social housing, a dental office, a community center, and a network of social enterprise businesses, all of which are specifically designed to attune to the ways of being of drug users. Through the practice of relational ethics and its political activity,

---

57.   Zigon 2019.

the DTES has become a new world attuned to itself because it is a world that is attuned to those and that which inhabit it. As attuned, this is an open world that lets its inhabitants be to become rather than impose a normative and *a priori* expectation, deviation from which results in exclusion.

One of the social enterprise businesses in the DTES is an artisan chocolate and coffee café that employs and trains residents of a nearby social housing unit for women, who are also drug users. Like the other social enterprises in the neighborhood, the chocolate café is organized to attune to the lives of its employees. This means, among other things, being flexible with scheduling, taking a nonjudgmental approach to work experience and discipline, and viewing a job not as an end in itself, but as an opening to other possibilities for being-in-the-world.

This opening has been described to me by Teresa, one of the employees of the café, as well as others in the DTES, as allowing possibilities of connection or being-with-others for those who find themselves there. In addition to connecting persons, the café, as with the bank and the other social enterprises of the DTES, also connects people to possibilities that have become available within the DTES, for example, different housing opportunities, various therapeutics or medical attention, events and activities, other jobs, or further education. This café, then, is not simply a profit-driven enterprise but primarily there as a nonjudgmental site of potentiality that lets its employees be, and in so doing allows them to become relationally connected and attuned to others as well as to a world built specifically for dwelling. In other words, the political project of building an attuned world has also made it possible for those who dwell there to become relationally ethical.

An example of how such sites of potentiality allow those who find themselves there to become relationally ethical is illustrated well by an afternoon I once spent with Teresa. After having just returned to Vancouver in the spring of 2015 from doing research in other locations, I went to the café for a coffee and to see if anyone I knew was working or just hanging out. After talking with a few people who were indeed there that day, Teresa, who was working in the back and heard from the manager that I was there, came out to give me a hug. We chatted for a few minutes. I gave her an update on my research, and she told me about how things had been with her since we last spoke. Most significantly, she told me that after being homeless for three years and then living several more years in the social housing unit for women, she was able to find her own apartment in subsidized housing on the other side of town. She immediately invited me over to see it, and, since it was just a few minutes from Stanley Park, to take a walk in the park together. Several days later I was knocking on her apartment door. Teresa let me in, and after showing me her studio apartment for a minute or so, she asked me: "can I get you anything? Tranquilizers, aspirin, weed, acid, coke?"

For many this likely seems a very strange and perhaps inappropriate question. But I would like to suggest that this, in fact, is a question that is indicative of relational ethics. For as I will show, it is a question that indicates Teresa's hospitality and attuned care for me as an enigmatic other who has just arrived. As she articulates with the first question, Teresa is trying to make me feel welcome. She is offering me "anything" within her capacity to give. As one who has arrived to where she has already been, she feels obliged to give me what I need to feel welcome with her. In other words, with this simple question she is already beginning to enact the hospitality and attuned care by which we can be-together-comfortably.

But the full expression of this attuned care only comes with the second question: "Tranquilizers, aspirin, weed, acid, coke?" For anyone who knows a bit about drug use this will immediately seem like an odd collection of possibilities. Some, like weed and acid, could certainly go together well, others, like tranquilizers and cocaine, not so well. Aspirin seems like the odd one out altogether. But, as I hope to show, Teresa's offer of aspirin is the key to understanding the question.

It is important not to read Teresa's question too literally. Certainly, if I had wanted any of these and more, I know that Teresa had them to give, and she would have. Despite this fact, however, the intent of the question, I want to suggest, was not a mere matter of fulfilling my potential desire to take a drug but, much more importantly, to enact attuned care. How is this so?

First, by offering this diverse range of possible substances Teresa is letting-me-be whomever it is that I may be or become as he who has arrived. Because the substances she offered are so diverse, each having their distinct effect, my response will indicate whom and how it is that I am at that moment and how this being-now may proceed. Second, by making such an offer, Teresa is also in the process of becoming attuned to me, for my response will allow her to respond to me in certain ways. For example, if I had accepted her offer of acid, our way of being-together in the park that day would have been very different, and she would have attuned accordingly. Third, and following from the second, her attunement allows me, in turn, to become attuned to her, and this co-attunement is another way of articulating the relational process of how it is that two beings become intertwined as the multiple singularity of being-with in a between that constitutes them both.

For being-with is not a "natural" process, and neither is it two individuals simply standing alongside one another. Rather, being-with, and the care that conditions it, is a hermeneutic process of co-attunement, by which those who happen to come alongside one another must attune to become-with-one-another in the between they now share. In other words, through these two simple questions, Teresa enacted a relational ethics by which co-attunement became possible in the between opened by them.

Teresa offering the "aspirin," I want to suggest, is key to understanding these questions as opening the between that allowed for our co-attunement. Aspirin clearly does not belong with the other options she offers. In this context, I read "aspirin" as the placeholder, the X factor, the etcetera of the hospitable offer. In other words, to offer me "aspirin" in this context is more or less equivalent to saying something like: "or anything else you might need and that I can provide." And this "anything else," I suggest, is another way of saying: "you are welcome in this place, you can feel comfortable here, and because we are being-here-together let's care for one another in whatever way becomes necessary," which of course would be very strange to say, so instead Teresa just offers me "aspirin." "Aspirin," then, in this instance is the signifier of attuned care as the necessary accompaniment of being-with.

What this example of a simple interaction shows is a very particular and singular instance of how the nonjudgment of harm reduction practice has dispersed effects in a broader world beyond the immediacy of a center or the café. My contention is that Teresa, as others I have written about, has become relationally ethical because her everyday life has become one significantly conditioned by the nonjudgment of harm reduction and the relational ethics and politics it can enact. From such sites of potentiality as the café, Teresa has come to embody a relational way of being with others. Then, as she responds to the enigmatic demand of singular situations by attuning and caring for that which opens between her and others, she further disperses her relationality and sensibility into her world. Through such openness, attunement, and care, relational ethics becomes a new norm.

The political transformation of the DTES enacted by means of relational ethics created the conditions for Teresa becoming who she is today. Such an ethics begins with a demand that emerges from a situation within which one finds oneself with others, a demand that pulls one out of oneself to respond in a modality of concern and care for the between where we dwell together. Through the enactment of the nonjudgment of harm reduction, political actors in the DTES responded to the ethical demand of their situation and built a world more attuned with itself and its inhabitants, such that how it is between them and those who live there is, for now, a place where they can dwell together.

Some Closing Words

Ethics, politics, and ontology must be thought together. How the *being* of the ethical subject is conceived goes a long way in determining how others, ethical relations, as well as ethical and political aims and concerns are conceived. I have tried to show that a relational ethics does just this by recognizing that the ethical subject is constituted by an ecstatic relationality of transcendence; this is so because such relationality structures not just social existence but existence as such.

If this relational ontology is accepted, then it follows that relational ethics can no longer recycle the same old concepts of traditional moral philosophy characterized by totality and the reduction of difference to sameness by means of projection and thematization. That is, we can no longer—as Hannah Arendt once put it[58]—hang on to the bannisters of such concepts as dignity, respect, right, and good, because these express an ontology that is fundamentally nonrelational. Rather, a relational ethics would instead take up such concepts as ecstatic relationality, breakdowns, attunement, dwelling, and letting-be as indicative of ethical experience. Such indicative concepts, at the very least, allow us to break free of thinking the self-sameness of a procedural individual, and take seriously the demand placed upon us by situations and those others there with us.

Indeed, a similar critical challenge could be offered to anthropology in general. The discipline is ripe for a moment of intense concept creation.[59] While there is little doubt that many have recently worked hard to move the discipline beyond its neo-Kantian foundations,[60] nevertheless,

---

58.   Arendt 2018: 473.

59.   For example: Zigon 2014a, 2015, 2018. See also Mattingly 2019.

60.   For example: Stewart 2007; Povinelli 2011, 2016; Holbraad and Pedersen 2017; Mazzarella 2017; S. McLean 2017.

the conceptual assumptions and apparatuses still dominant within anthropology remain tethered to these foundations. As I have argued elsewhere, concepts come with a conceptual proclivity acquired over long-time use,[61] and so even our best intentions of redefining concepts often fail. Many of the discipline's most dearly held concepts—society, culture, or kinship, for example—may have made sense in the fragmented world of nationalism and colonialism in the heyday of fin-de-siècle neo-Kantianism. But today our concepts must do justice to the complexity of the intertwined global, ecological, and human relationality that characterizes the contemporary condition. That is, our time demands a sustained project of concept creation—ontological, political, and ethical—that is adequate to our contemporary condition of ecstatically relational existence. This chapter and those that follow are an attempt to do just that in ontological and ethical terms.

61. Zigon 2018.

CHAPTER 2

Truth, Thinking, Ethics

How is it between us? Today it is said that the contemporary condition is increasingly one of post-truth. How should one respond to such a claim? We might begin by querying the very possibility of a *between* in a condition of post-truth. Can there be a between that gives way to us under conditions of post-truth? Put another way: is there a possibility for *us* to emerge in conditions of post-truth, or are persons left as solitary and isolated individuals incapable of connecting with others and their worlds? Does post-truth foreclose witness? And if so, is there any possibility of reconnecting, to regain the essential witness that is the condition for us becoming who we are?

In 2016 Oxford Languages named post-truth its word of the year. In doing so, it defined post-truth as "relating to or denoting circumstances in which objective facts are less influential in shaping public opinion than appeals to emotion and personal belief."[1] Notice that truth is here equated with "objective facts," or, better put, the correspondence between "objective facts" and a human subject and its propositions. This is, to say the least, an extremely narrow and insipid, and one is tempted to say not very human, notion of truth. It is, however, a common definition of truth, and particularly so among philosophers of the analytic variety. Simon Critchley recalls his former teacher once saying: "Truth isn't interesting.

---

1. Oxford Languages, "Word of the Year 2016." https://languages.oup.com/word-of-the-year/2016/.

If you want truth, open a phonebook."[2] Indeed. Critchley's teacher surely had the correspondence theory of truth in mind when he said this.

One is inclined to ask: when was it that emotion and personal belief was not more influential on public opinion than objective facts? Here we need simply refer to such phenomena as religion and nationalism (even the benign sort) to call into question the apparent assumption behind this definition that at some point in the not very distant past public opinion was shaped predominantly (or entirely?) by clear and distinct truths understood as correspondence to objective facts. History suggests otherwise. Rather than post-truth as the new and disturbing feature of our time, perhaps instead the very idea that truth should be equated with "objective facts" is most concerning.

It is understandable how this came about. Over the course of the past 150 years within the so-called Western world, God died and secularism spread, two world wars crushed any good faith belief in Enlightenment ideals, and the capitalist machine transformed the planet into a resource for profit-seeking individuals. Under such conditions, truth and those with a recognized authority to uphold or spread it have increasingly been considered illegitimate. Except, that is, for science and scientists—though, of course, these too have recently been questioned by some in the public domain.

Still, it is difficult to deny that for many today, science remains the authority on truth. Since at least the Second World War, science has increasingly become technology obsessed and instrumentarian focused; and because much of what counts today as scientific discovery has been redefined in terms of profit-driven innovation as a result of its unholy alliance with the capitalist machine,[3] science today has become one of the foundations upholding the idea of truth as objective fact.[4] This is, perhaps, most clearly seen in the increasing influence of so-called data science, which not only is very comfortably allied with finance capitalism, but also understands the "truth" revealed by data as little more than facts, and science as little more than the technologically efficient reproduction of those facts. When the "truth" of these facts, however, are regularly

---

2. Simon Critchley, "Truth." Apply-Degger (podcast, episode 10). https://www.onassis.org/channel/apply-degger-podcast-simon-critchley (accessed July 10, 2020).

3. For an outstanding analysis of this, see P. Scherz 2019.

4. Porter 1995; Daston and Galison 2010.

characterized by injustice and inequality, perhaps these "truths" ought not be reproduced.[5] This is a topic to be addressed in the next chapter.

Nevertheless, Oxford Languages supports its choice by claiming that post-truth is not "an isolated quality of particular assertions," but rather "a general characteristic of our age."[6] Put another way: the claim is that we live in times conditioned by post-truth. While that may indeed be the case, considering this condition unique to our time necessitates a particularly Euro-American understanding of history, or perhaps even more specifically, an Anglo-American understanding. For one need not look very far or wide in time or geography to find other examples that might also be characterized as post-truth conditions. Indeed, a good deal of the twentieth century could be precisely characterized as just this, and located right there in the center, as well as the periphery, of Europe. I refer, of course, to Nazi Germany and the Soviet Union and its various satellites.

Hannah Arendt remains today the most significant thinker of the relation between truth and totalitarian politics. In *The Origins of Totalitarianism*, Arendt writes that one of the primary characteristics of this form of politics is "that gigantic lies and monstrous falsehoods can eventually be established as unquestioned facts ... and that the difference between truth and falsehood may cease to be objective and become a mere matter of power and cleverness, of pressure and infinite repetition."[7] Importantly, Arendt makes the essential point that it is not the convinced Nazi, for example, who is the ideal subject of totalitarian politics, but rather ordinary "people for whom the distinction between fact and fiction (i.e., the reality of experience) and the distinction between true and false (i.e., the standards of thought) no longer exist."[8] Ordinary people in their everyday lives become susceptible to this way of being, according to Arendt, when they are increasingly isolated from one another.

The atomized, isolated, lonely individual is most vulnerable to what is now called post-truth politics. Above all, it is the consequence of this vulnerability that is of great concern. In our contemporary condition

---

5. For just a few examples of a growing literature on the reproduction of injustices and inequalities by algorithms and big data, see: O'Neil 2016; Cheney-Lippold 2017; Noble 2018.

6. Oxford Languages, "Word of the Year 2016." https://languages.oup.com/word-of-the-year/2016/.

7. Arendt 1973: 333.

8. Arendt 1973: 474.

characterized by such loneliness and the consequential increase of addiction, anxiety, and despair, where "social interaction" is most regularly done by means of fragmentary social media posts, all of which is supported by a neoliberalism that only recognizes persons as self-responsible and autonomous individuals, and which too often results in persons becoming selfish individuals, it is no wonder that the very possibility of a between that gives way to us is increasingly foreclosed by totalitarian-like politics.

In such a condition, we must ask: what is to be done? Indeed, much of the concern today about post-truth revolves precisely around the potential rise of, if not totalitarian politics, then certainly authoritarian politics. To begin to address the question of what is to be done, it will be helpful first to consider an historical example of a similar condition of "post-truth" and authoritarian/totalitarian politics, and query as to how those living in such a condition responded. How was it that in isolating conditions of post-truth some were still able to connect with others, and in so doing, slowly bring about an otherwise?

Live Within Truth

In his famous essay, "The Power of the Powerless," the playwright, dissident, and eventual first president of post-Communist Czechoslovakia, Václav Havel, articulates his political, ethical, and existential imperative "to live within the truth."[9] Written in 1978, this essay was his response to life under the Czechoslovakian Communist regime—a condition that today would be called post-truth. At first glance, this imperative seems rather straightforward, particularly when contrasted with how Havel describes the opposite, that is, "living within a lie." Such a distinction surely conjures Arendt's claim that totalitarianism is a form of politics in which "the difference between truth and falsehood may cease to be objective and become a mere matter of power and cleverness, of pressure and infinite repetition."

While this is as good a description as any for understanding how ideology is made the "truth" of everyday life under certain regimes of power, such a manner of putting it, nevertheless, too easily slips into an overly banal notion of truth as equivalent with objective fact, such that, for example, the number of persons attending a presidential inauguration becomes a primary battleground over the truthfulness of a regime.

---

9.   Havel 1992.

It matters, of course, whether leaders can speak honestly about simple phenomena in the world like the number of people at an event, let alone more complex phenomena such as the economy or public health. Still, dishonesty by politicians alone cannot be the standard by which we define the limits of totalitarianism, for surely, if it were, we would know no other form of politics.

Havel's distinction between living within truth or living within a lie, in contrast, is a matter of one's *comportment* within what he calls the panorama of everyday life. In other words, Havel is not writing about—or at least not primarily so—the veracity of this or that statement, but rather how one *is* with one's world. To live within the truth rather than living within a lie is a matter of being *dispositionally attuned* to the panorama of everyday life, or what I suggest in the final section of this chapter is better considered in terms of the sense of the world.

Again, this is not a matter of the truth or falsity of one's propositional statements—whether the greengrocer, to use Havel's famous example, is attempting to articulate something objectively true about the world and his relation to it when he hangs the "Workers of the world, unite!" sign in his shop window. But rather, to live within truth is a matter of one's moral comportment with the world, how we "address the world," a matter of "responsibility to and for the world," and as such, has as its "proper point of departure ... concern [and care] for others."[10] The articulation of such a moral disposition—or what I call in the next section embodied morality—Havel attributes to the Czech phenomenologist Jan Patočka with the latter's saying that "the most interesting thing about responsibility is that we carry it with us everywhere."[11] Put another way, we might call this an embodied commitment to responsively attune to the world and those others there with us.

In his otherwise brilliant ethnographic and theoretical description of the performative shift of late socialism's authoritative discourse, the anthropologist Alexei Yurchak misreads Havel's argument when he critiques the latter for articulating a correspondence theory of propositional truth. Utilizing the conceptual language of J. L. Austin's theory of performatives, Yurchak argues that Havel is too narrowly concerned with the constative dimension of language—the conveyance of meaning that is either a true or false description of facts—in contrast to the performative dimension—the felicitous or infelicitous force of language that is

---

10.   Havel 1992: 147, 194, 195.
11.   Havel 1992: 195.

neither true nor false but rather does something in the world.[12] While Yurchak very convincingly shows that this latter performative dimension of language best describes the condition of late socialism, he mistakenly attributes a focus on the constative dimension of language to Havel. Admittedly, it is rather easy to read Havel in this way, considering his rhetorical contrast between living within truth and living within a lie, and this reading is made even more understandable considering that the genre of dissident writing is perhaps most obviously read as articulating certain truths over and against the lies of a totalitarian regime. Nevertheless, Havel's essay is more sophisticated than your run-of-the-mill dissident treatise, and it is precisely the existential phenomenological undercurrent of the essay that makes it so.

For Havel is *not* an analytic philosopher soul-numbingly obsessed with the most logical argument to support, for example, that the statement "'snow is white' is true iff it corresponds to the fact that snow is white" is more truthful than "'snow is white' is true iff snow is white," or vice versa.[13] Far from it. Rather, Havel is an existentialist; and for this reason, he does not define truth in terms of, for example, a correspondence between a subject and objective facts, but rather in terms of a dispositional manner of being. Put another way, when Havel writes about living within the truth, he is primarily and for the most part writing about the human existential need to dwell openly in a world together with others. As Havel puts it, there is a "human predisposition to truth" or an "openness to truth."[14] Indeed, it is only because of this predisposition to truth, so claims Havel, that it becomes possible to live a lie.

This notion of truth and the human predisposition and openness to truth is above all a Heideggerian notion. For Heidegger, the full existential and ontological meaning of his claim that "Dasein is in the truth" is that Dasein is also "in untruth."[15] Importantly, then, to be human—to be Dasein—is *to be* the movement between truth and untruth. Again, this is not a philosophical claim about the capacity to utter correspondingly true or false propositions. Rather, to be the movement between truth and untruth is a matter of comportment, or better put, dispositional

---

12. Yurchak 2006: 19.
13. David 2020. Note that "iff" is an abbreviation for "if and only if."
14. Havel 1992: 148.
15. Heidegger 1996: 204. Although it is more complicated than this, in *Being and Time* Heidegger more or less equates Dasein with the being we normally call human.

attunement.[16] Heidegger seeks to move beyond the Cartesian and Kantian subject that stands over and against objects and its world by looking to the ancient Greek conception of truth as *alētheia*, which he translates as unconcealment. If the Cartesian/Kantian subject agentively attempts to project knowledge onto objects and the world such that this projection corresponds "truthfully" with the latter, then truth as *alētheia* or unconcealment is the result of having a certain dispositional attunement with a particular object or world such that the latter is let be to show itself as itself. Thus, truth in this sense is neither in the subject nor in the object nor in their correspondence. Rather, truth is the relational attunement—the between—that allows an existent to show itself as itself and allows other existents to let that showing as unfolding happen.

It is for this reason, then, that Heidegger writes that the "essence of truth reveals itself as freedom." For only through freedom can attunement occur between existents in such a way as to let unconcealment unfold. This is so because freedom is not an agentive capacity for acting by means of a projection of what Levinas called the Same; rather freedom "lets beings be the beings they are" to disclose themselves as such. This freedom as letting be, Heidegger is quick to tell us, is not a matter of "neglect or indifference but rather the opposite. To let be is to engage oneself with beings."[17] Or as Havel put it, to live within truth is to be "concern[ed] [and care] for others."[18] This relational conception of concern and care prefigures the way in which many anthropologists today write about these—that is, that concern and care are a matter of cultivating moral dispositions for attuning with others in a shared world.[19] Thus, for example, in her ethnographic study of familial care for the aging in Thailand, Felicity Aulino shows that care is better conceived in terms of the ritualistic—that is, the embodied, repetitive, and correct—enactment of care practices rather than as the willful connection between one's motivations and one's actions.[20] Put another way, Aulino shows that in contrast to predominant Western conceptions of care that emphasize the intentions of a moral agent, care in Thailand is best understood in terms of what I call embodied morality.

---

16. Heidegger 2011b: 75.
17. Heidegger 2011b: 75, 72, 72.
18. Havel 1992: 195.
19. For example: Mattingly 2014; Aulino 2019; Zigon 2019; Shohet 2021; Tidey 2022.
20. Aulino 2019.

Rather than capacities of the subject to be agentively enacted, both freedom and truth—and therefore, concern and care as well—are indicative of an attuned relation between existents of the world. Therefore, "'truth' is not a feature of correct propositions that are asserted of an 'object' by a human 'subject' and then 'are valid' somewhere, in what sphere we know not; rather, *truth is disclosure of beings through which an openness essentially unfolds.*"[21]

Havel most certainly adopted his imperative to "live within truth" from this Heideggerian articulation and Heidegger's argument that "Dasein is in the truth."[22] But he likely did so through an interpretation of Heidegger by his mentor Jan Patočka, the Czech phenomenologist to whom Havel's essay was dedicated.[23] For Patočka, humans "are the only beings [that] can live in truth," by which he means "life in a relation to the world" rather than the anxiety of "roles and needs."[24] Not unlike Arendt's distinction between work and labor,[25] Patočka attempts to articulate the difference between an existentially meaningful and free intertwining with the world, what he and Havel call living within truth, and an existentially meaningless and unfree emplacement in a world as one with a "role" that is done simply to fulfill a "need." It is this latter condition that for both Patočka and Havel leads to living a lie; not because it is a false correspondence but because it is fundamentally antithetical to the kind of being humans are. For it is only by living in truth as a singularly "irreplaceable" being, Patočka tells us, that one is "at home with" oneself and dwells with others in a world of sense.[26]

Havel writes: "Between the aims of the [Czechoslovakian Communist regime] and the aims of life there is a yawning abyss: while life, in its essence, moves toward plurality, diversity, independent self-constitution, and self-organization, in short, toward the fulfillment of its own freedom, the [Czechoslovakian Communist] system demands conformity,

---

21. Heidegger 2011b: 74; italics added. The anthropologist Martin Holbraad has written of a very similar conception of truth. Holbraad writes that "there can be little doubt that the concept of truth that this book sets out to articulate could be arrived at by a philosophical route." Indeed, it would seem that Heidegger's route is precisely it. See Holbraad 2012: xx.
22. Heidegger 1996: 204.
23. Gubser 2014.
24. Patočka 1998: 177.
25. Arendt 1998.
26. Patočka 1998: 177.

uniformity, and discipline."[27] This is Havel's way of articulating Patočka's distinction between "life in a relation to the world" and the anxiety of "roles and needs." As in this quote, throughout the essay Havel continuously builds on Patočka in equating, or at least making an essential link between, truth and life. If truth is equated with life, or at least indicative thereof, then living within truth is precisely living freedom; living free *not* as an individualist bourgeois consumer and fulfiller of desire, but existentially as always open to the multifarious unfolding of existence as such.

Havel knows that the greengrocer "is indifferent to the semantic content"[28] of the sign he hangs, and only cares whether it shows his ritualistic adherence to what must be done in order not to stir the pot, as it were. Indeed, for the most part, Havel is not advocating that the greengrocer should stop hanging the sign. The real concern for Havel is what the greengrocer does now that he has hung the sign. Havel does not, of course, expect the greengrocer to become a dissident like himself and make speeches and organize strikes—though he may, and Havel would certainly support that. Rather, and ultimately, Havel urges the greengrocer to help build and participate in what he calls parallel structures of such seemingly minor activities as unsanctioned rock concerts or plays or informal organizations to address particular situational problems that may arise.[29]

These parallel structures are a "rudimentary prefiguration" of "open communities," Havel tells us.[30] Such "existential revolutions," as he also calls them, provide an opportunity for a "new experience of being," which gives way to the "rehabilitation of values like trust, openness, responsibility, solidarity, love," and thus a "moral reconstitution of society."[31] Similarly, in the context of the contemporary drug war and activism against it, I have called this a politics of worldbuilding.[32] Indeed, it was precisely the various forms this existential revolution and politics of worldbuilding took in the later years of the Czechoslovakian Communist regime that eventually gave way to the Velvet Revolution and the collapse of that regime.

---

27. Havel 1992: 134–35.
28. Havel 1992: 132.
29. Havel 1992: 192–94.
30. Havel 1992: 213.
31. Havel 1992: 209–10.
32. Zigon 2018.

With this more nuanced understanding of the influences and context of Havel's work, perhaps it is now easier to see that those concerts, café groups, and other forms of sociality that Yurchak describes as allowing for the rather quick and easy collapse of the Soviet Union were very similar to that which Havel describes as living within truth and the existential, moral, and political revolutions this attunement gives way to. While Yurchak relies on a theory of performativity to explain this collapse, perhaps we can now see that performativity may best be understood as indicative of the Heideggerian movement between truth and untruth as an attempt to become felicitously attuned to a world.[33]

Thinking

The writings of Havel—and eventually Yurchak—were vital for me in the early years of my development of the ethnographic theory of relational ethics I am here presenting. For it was just this question of how to morally live within truth that drew me to do ethnographic research in Russia in the late 1990s and early 2000s. During those so-called transition years, it was not difficult to find media discourse or hear people in their everyday conversations claim that Russians had lost their moral bearing. And this moral disorientation was often connected to questions of truth in relation to both the former Soviet regime and its new neoliberal replacement. Russia during this period, therefore, offered a time and place to study how it is that persons living through what I would come to call a societal-wide breakdown ethically respond by reattuning their relations with one another and their newly emerging world. In other words, Russia at this time offered the perfect opportunity to research the relation between ethics and truth and how this relation was lived in ordinary everyday life. In the rest of this chapter, I will begin to delineate the notions of embodied morality, moral breakdown, and ethics that emerged from this ethnographic research.[34]

---

33. For example, Simon Critchley offers an interesting interpretation of Heidegger's notions of repetition, anticipatory resoluteness, care, and selfhood in terms of performativity. See Critchley, "Anticipatory Resoluteness." Apply-Degger (podcast, episode 13) (accessed September 18, 2020); Heidegger 1996: sections 62–64.

34. See, for example, Zigon 2010, also 2007, 2009a.

As a result of that research project, I came to understand human life as the movement between truth and untruth in just the way described in the previous section. Therefore, a leading question for me was: if human life is the movement between truth and untruth, and one's disposition or comportment with the world is fundamental for how one *is* in this movement, then how can we account for the coming-to-be of a disposition that is adequate to truth? Put another way: what is the process by which one becomes capable of living within truth such that the possibility of untruth is not eliminated—for this is impossible in any aletheiological constellation of the movement between truth and untruth—but that one *become capable of recognizing* attunement with truth rather than untruth? My response was: to think.

Hannah Arendt's work on thinking is vital here. Recall that Arendt did not consider the evil deeds of the Nazi Eichmann in terms of the demonic, but rather in terms of banality.[35] Eichmann, like so many other Nazis,[36] committed evil acts not because he was a monster, but because he was thoughtless. Thoughtlessness, Arendt is quick to remind us, is not stupidity. For although Arendt is adamant that all humans are capable of thinking—indeed, at one point she defines humans as thinking beings—she is also clear that sometimes very intelligent people simply do not do so. Furthermore, Arendt insists that in our everyday lives of going about our daily activities with one another we do not think. This is a view of the human that she shares with perhaps the two most significant philosophers of the twentieth century—Martin Heidegger and Ludwig Wittgenstein.[37] In contrast to the brain-centric view of the human that considers all human activity in terms of cognitive thinking of some order or another, Arendt considers everyday life more in terms of habits than mind. Still, for Arendt it is those moments of stepping away from the habitual flow of the everyday, when we "stop and think," that is the essence of humanness.[38] For it is precisely because of such moments, she contends, that we can judge such things as good and beauty. Indeed, it was her observations of Eichmann and her connection of thoughtlessness to evil that led her to ask an important question for ethical theory: "Might the problem of good and evil, our

---

35. Arendt 2006.
36. See, for example, Browning 1998.
37. Braver 2014: chapter 4.
38. Arendt 1978: 4.

faculty for telling right from wrong, be connected with our faculty of thought?"[39]

Her response is yes. But not because thinking offers us the "right" answer to our ethical dilemma. Arendt is clear: thinking does not produce anything. Neither can thinking be applied—either universally or situationally—in our everyday lives. When we "stop and think" we do not discover a moral law or principle or criterion according to which we should act, thus guaranteeing us moral standing. Neither, it should be added, does thinking produce truth or knowledge. In a quite literal way, nothing—no-thing—is produced by thought. If this is so, then how is it—my research compelled me to ask—that thinking is central to ethics?

Much of our everyday life is lived without thought, and embodied habit—or what could also be called an active disposition—better describes how it is that we are in our worlds together. One's habituated disposition is the consequence of having lived a uniquely relational existential trajectory, and as such it is not hyperbole to say that each of us is uniquely singular. Yet, because most of those with whom we normally interact in our everyday lives have had very similar existential trajectories, oftentimes each of our singular embodied dispositions are so similar that we tend to understand them as "shared."

Thus, my ethnographic research strongly suggested that what in social and cultural theory tends to be understood in terms of sharedness—for example, by means of the culture concept—or in ethical theory tends to be understood in terms of a universally shared morality—even if this is relativized to a shared cultural morality—is ethnographically better understood in terms of the ethically interpretive work done in social life to cover over the gaps of difference. Put another way, everyday social life is possible because of the hermeneutic work each of us does to cover over the infinite gap between our unique singularities. This hermeneutic movement between "sharedness" and singularity entails that unlike explanations of human action that posit sharedness as sameness or equivalency, everyday social life is better understood in terms of "sharedness" in scare quotes, which is perhaps better described as shades of similarity.

This phenomenological-hermeneutic understanding of embodied habit as the primary modality of being in everyday life does not mean, however, that "thoughts" do not run through our "mind." Of course, they do. But these "thoughts"—like our bodily actions—are better considered in terms of dispositions. Just as our bodies habitually move in

---

39.   Arendt 1978: 5.

certain ways in certain situations—offering a hand when first meeting someone—so too do our "thoughts." So too, it should be noted, does our speech—"nice to meet you," one might habitually say while offering their hand. And just as our bodies move and speak in ways that are at once "shared" with others and yet singularly unique to our specific existential trajectory, so too are our "thoughts."

This dispositional modality of living everyday life in a mostly smooth and unquestioned manner—let's call it living in an existentially comfortable manner—is what I call embodied morality.[40] To live with existential comfort in our everyday dispositional mode does *not* mean, for example, to have a "comfortable confidence of being able routinely to do the right thing," or a psychologized, or even and especially a bourgeois sense of feeling comfortable.[41] Rather, by existential comfort I intend an effortless absorption in a world as one's everyday way of being. Indeed, anxiety might be just as likely the mood of this effortless absorption as is "confidence." The etymological root of comfort helps us see it as a possible ethical concept. For the Latin root of comfort (*com-fortis*) would be rendered something like strength together, or communal fortitude, or perseverance, revealing to us how existential comfort as the aim of ethics is not only something always achieved with others, but also a modality of being that is not necessarily anything like a "good" traditionally conceived but rather one of withness.

This dispositional way of being in the world—one's embodied morality—is enacted smoothly and unquestionably—comfortably—because one has become attuned to one's world and those others there with you. If asked "how is it between us?" one might reply unthinkingly: "good." Such a response does not indicate that the between is in any "objective" sense "good"—however that may be determined—but rather that the attuned withness of our embodied moral way of being with one another is (more or less) smoothly—because unnoticeably—unfolding.

Thus, while this embodied moral way of being may manifest as familial care for the ethnographic interlocutors of anthropologists such as Felicity Aulino or Sylvia Tidey,[42] for many of my Russian interlocutors it manifested more as anxiety in relation to both others and their shared world. This is so because of the societal-wide breakdown that characterized the first decade of post-Soviet Russia that I described

40.   Zigon 2007, 2009a, 2011, 2018, 2019.
41.   Laidlaw 2014: 124–29.
42.   Aulino 2019; Tidey 2022.

at the beginning of this section. In a world characterized above all by change and disruption, disorientation and questioning, anxiety became for many of my interlocutors their everyday dispositional way of being, whereby a general sense of uncertainty and instability of meaning, value, and identity became the everyday norm. Embodied morality, then, is just one's average everyday way of being in the world with others, whoever or whatever those others may be, and however that embodied habit may have developed.

Notice that this notion of embodied morality does not necessarily entail that there is anything particularly "good" about one's everyday way of being-with. Arendt is clear on this matter: while everyday lives may be lived mostly in the modality of a habituated disposition, such habits can be changed rather easily for better or worse.[43] The example she uses to illustrate this is how quickly average Germans and Russians were able to change their habituated everyday way of being—their embodied moral-ity—along with the newly imposed Nazi and Soviet regimes. If a German wished to respond to the question of "how is it between us?" with the answer "good," then this entailed the adoption of a different embod-ied morality with which to dispositionally keep going. This is something, so it seemed to Arendt, that Eichmann did easily and thoughtlessly. In-deed, for Arendt, the ease with which so many Germans and Russians quickly and, to all appearances seamlessly, adjusted to the new regimes, makes clear that dispositions as such are no deterrent against evil. It was precisely the ease with which they could be adjusted that Arendt consid-ered in terms of thoughtlessness.

Dispositional or embodied morality, then, is *not* ethics. Rather, eth-ics occurs when there is a moral breakdown, when a dissonance arises between a dispositional normativity and its founding exclusion, thus forcing one to reflect on and alter one's already acquired way of being in the world to account for this discord. In other words, ethics occurs when one is compelled to think. As Arendt put it, thinking "interrupts any doing, any ordinary activities, no matter what they happen to be. All thinking demands a *stop*-and-think." Thus, Arendt emphasizes, think-ing indicates an "*out of order.*"[44] It must be noted, however, that when a moral breakdown occurs and ethics begins, the "stop-and-think" of ethics does not entail a rupturing of the everyday, though there is, of

---

43. Arendt 1978: 177.
44. Arendt 1978: 78; italics in original.

course, an interruption of ordinary activity and a stepping-away from one's dispositional mode of being.

Being clear about this distinction between a rupture and an interruption of the everyday is important. For a moral breakdown does *not* force one to run into a secluded nonsocial space to be alone with one's thoughts, and *neither* does one become frozen, object-like, as the world continues all around. It does, however, compel one to stop and think—is this really what I want to be doing or saying right now?—and to step away from one's habit—to notice that what I'm doing or saying right now could indeed be otherwise—and thus, to *critically* assess how I could act, speak, and be differently. All of this *can be done and is done* right there in the continuing midst of everyday life.

One example from my research that I have written about in more detail elsewhere is of Aleksandra Vladimirovna, who having just arrived at the train station in time to jump on a train without first buying a ticket, and then never having been approached by a conductor to buy one on the train, became perplexed as to what she should do.[45] As an Orthodox Christian, she felt that she was being dishonest by not paying for a ticket, and yet no conductor was to be found. There amid the hustle and bustle of a busy train she thought about how to respond. She prayed on it. She considered various options of what she could do. But she also spoke with some sitting near her about their day and the ride. She also looked forward to her time away from the city. In other words, she engaged in thinking about her ethical dilemma while still there in the unfolding midst of everyday life with all its ordinary social interactions and anticipations. Eventually, after disembarking, she gave the amount of a train ticket to a beggar.

The point I want to make is that rather than a rupture from the ordinary, the thinking that characterizes a moral breakdown initiates a more intensely felt and considered relational intertwining; and this relationality is more intensely felt and considered in the moment of breakdown precisely because the demand of the situation has explicitly called "me" to think and, ultimately, to ethically attune. Aleksandra Vladimirovna remained engaged in her ordinary life while at the same time thinking through how best to attune to the situation that she found herself in. The moment of moral breakdown, then, is that ethical moment when one experiences most intensely the demand to care and attend to the

---

45. Zigon 2010.

constitutive relational intertwining that gives way to us, and this care and attending occurs as thinking.

What called Aleksandra Vladimirovna to think? Indeed, what calls any of us to think? This is a question posed by Heidegger in his lecture course *Was Heißt Denken?* Although this is normally translated as *What is Called Thinking?*, the wordplay of *heißen* allows the title to be alternatively translated as *What Calls Out to Thinking?* or *What Calls Upon Thinking?* Or, as I pose the question: what calls us to think? Heidegger's answer, in short, is that what calls us to think is that which is thought.[46] This phenomenological conception of thinking contrasts with the dominant conception of thinking as cognitive, the view that thinking originates in the brain and has as its material, as it were, mere images or representations of its object of thought in the world. Heidegger's phenomenological conception of thinking, on the other hand, understands thinking as originating in that which demands—or calls out—to be thought. That is, thinking originates in the thing or matter or situation itself.

Some thing or matter or situation in the world calls out to us—it places a demand upon us—to which one must respond. One can, of course, ignore the call. That is, one can simply not think and continue with one's dispositional mode of being. But as Bernhard Waldenfels puts it, even this nonresponse is a response.[47] In other words, one may not heed the call to think, but the demand to respond to the call cannot be ignored. If one does respond in the modality of thought, however, that which calls us to think pulls us beyond ourselves such that thinking is always an ecstatically relational experience of thinking *with* the thing, matter, or situation itself. Thinking, then, happens in the world; rather than indicating a distanced observation, thinking entails a more intense relational intertwining with that which calls us to it.

Similarly, a moral breakdown is initiated by an ethical demand placed upon one by another person, situation, or event. This ethical demand cannot be ignored: one must respond. For example, the situation of not having paid for a ticket placed a demand upon Aleksandra Vladimirovna, which she experienced as moral breakdown, and thus she ethically responded with first thought and then action. Note, however, that how one responds is vital for answering the question of how it is between us. One can, for example, ignore the ethical demand and continue in one's dispositional mode of being. This, however, is precisely that with

---

46. Heidegger 1968.
47. Waldenfels 2011.

which Arendt was so concerned. For this is the thoughtless response that always runs the risk of laying the foundation for evil, an evil which itself becomes dispositional. Alternatively, one can—as did Aleksandra Vladimirovna—heed the call of the ethical demand, experience a moral breakdown, and step away from one's dispositional everydayness to stop and think. One can respond to the ethical demand by *becoming* an ethical being.

Conceiving of ethics in terms of moral breakdowns that respond to ethical demands has become a hallmark of various anthropological contributions to ethical theory, even when such breakdowns go by other names. Thus, for example, Sarah Pinto, writing about women and madness in India, articulates an ethics of dissolution as an ethics that "focuses on relations, especially their undoing," and a concern for "the habitation of breakdown as much as (or more than) on making anew (or remaking)." Similarly, Joel Robbins coined the term moral torment to describe temporally extended periods of breakdown among the Urapmin of Papua New Guinea; Cheryl Mattingly, writing about African-American families caring for chronically ill children, has coined the term moral laboratories to describe ethical striving during morally problematic periods; and Michael Lambek has contrasted explicit ethics to the more ordinary tacit ethics of everyday life.[48] Thus, in contrast to the critique of breakdown as causing a rupture with social life, each of these theoretical contributions help us see that moments of breakdown are in fact characterized as a more intense relationality with a morally fraught situation.

Thinking, then, as that which one does in ethical moments of moral breakdown, pulls us ever more tightly into the world. We are most intensely relational when we ethically think in moments of breakdown. This is so not only as one goes beyond oneself to the thing or situation to be thought, but also, as Arendt insists, as one goes within oneself. For while Heidegger emphasizes the call of thinking—that pull that brings one ecstatically *beyond* oneself—Arendt emphasizes the internal dialogue of thinking—that pull that brings one ecstatically *within* oneself. Thinking manifests what Arendt calls the two-in-one, or the duality of being human.[49]

In normal everyday life, Arendt claims, the human is One. We can think of this being One in terms of our everyday dispositional way of being—our embodied morality. But when one is called to think, a split

---

48.   Pinto 2014: 4, 257; Robbins 2004; Mattingly 2014; Lambek 2010a.
49.   Arendt 1978: 185.

occurs such that One becomes two, and a silent internal dialogue ensues between me and myself. Put another way, one becomes relationally intertwined with oneself. Arendt linked her description of thinking with an experience of conscience. But perhaps this ecstatic relationality of thinking that pulls one both into and beyond oneself simultaneously is better considered in terms of Heidegger's call of conscience, which he describes as a call coming *"from* me, and yet *over* me."[50] This is a call, it should be noted, that demands that one step away from one's dispositional everydayness (what Heidegger called *Das Man*, often translated as the they-self) in response to a situation of moral breakdown.[51]

Thinking, then, is the most relational modality of being human in that it entails at one and the same time an ecstatic relationality with the thing, matter, or situation that calls for thought, *and* an ecstatic relationality with oneself as the two-in-one. Thinking, in this sense, is that which is most indicative of ontological withness, and, therefore, that which is most necessary for allowing a between to emerge. As Jean-Luc Nancy puts it, thought allows for the very structure of existence because it is that which *"ex-tends* the play of differences by which we exist in the relation of singularities."[52]

This is so because thinking "is for us what is most free."[53] This link between thinking and freedom is essential for ethics. Arendt was clear about this link: thinking frees "an open space of moral or aesthetic discrimination and discernment."[54] Such thinking in moments of moral breakdown, then, is critical thinking in that "we constantly raise the basic Socratic question: *What do you mean when you say...?*"[55] We could add the equally critical question: "Why is it that you do that?"

Importantly, such critical thinking does not produce the new moral law or principle that we can then apply to the situation that demands us to think, let alone apply it universally. Rather, thinking is deconstructive. It "purges us of 'fixed habits of thought, ossified rules and standards,' and 'conventional, standardized codes of expression.'"[56] In other words,

---

50. Heidegger 1996: 254; italics in original.
51. Heidegger 1996: sections 54–57.
52. Nancy 1993: 104; italics in original.
53. Nancy 1993: 172.
54. Beiner 1982: 112.
55. Arendt 1978: 185; italics in original.
56. Villa 1999: 89.

thinking as an essentially deconstructive capacity frees one to respond to the singularity of the situation that has called one to think. Or as Mattingly might put it, thinking allows us to defrost our concepts in response to perplexing particulars.[57] Or, as Arendt so pointedly put it, "thinking means that each time you are confronted with some difficulty in life you have to make up your mind anew."[58]

It is interesting to note that Michel Foucault articulated a very similar relation between thought, freedom, critique, and ethics—one that has become rather influential within the anthropology of ethics, and most particularly so as interpreted by James Laidlaw.[59] Thus, for example, Foucault distinguished thought from more habituated modes of conduct, and considered the former as a critical assessment of the latter. Thought, he said, "is what allows one to step back from this [habituated] way of acting or reacting, to present it to oneself as an object of thought and to question it as to its meaning, its conditions, and its goals. Thought is freedom in relation to what one does, the motion by which one detaches oneself from it, establishes it as an object, and reflects on it as a problem."[60] Thinking in moments of moral breakdown—or what Foucault here calls stepping back—clears a space, as it were, for responding to the singularity of the ethical demand free of habituated convention.[61] In other words, it is precisely the freedom to think that a moral breakdown allows that makes possible a critical perspective on oneself and one's world. Put another way, it is the moral breakdown that opens the possibility for political action.

Sense of the World

The philosopher Anne O'Byrne's critical response to the longtime focus of hermeneutics on meaning can, I suggest, equally respond to the so-called West's longtime fascination with truth. For whether one speaks of meaning or truth, surely O'Byrne is onto something when she writes that there is "a worry that clings to [these terms], an anxiety that what

---

57. Mattingly 2019.
58. Arendt 1978: 177.
59. Laidlaw 2002, 2014 .
60. Foucault 1997: 117.
61. See Løgstrup 1997.

really matters is not here but elsewhere."[62] For indeed the conceptual proclivity of "truth" or "meaning" has become such that try as we might, just saying the word conjures the braincentric view of being-human, along with all of its Cartesian baggage of correspondence, mental representations, and rational implications. Most certainly, then, "what really matters is not here but elsewhere." O'Byrne suggests instead that a carnal hermeneutics—a bodied hermeneutics as the ongoing interpretation of the intertwined and knotted materiality of the world—entails instead an indicative concept such as sense.[63]

Engaging with Jean-Luc Nancy's conception of sense, O'Byrne writes that "sense cannot be given in advance but comes to be in the worldliest way, *between us.*"[64] Indeed, as Nancy writes: "Truth punctuates, sense enchains."[65] Put another way: truth is that which individuates and separates—truth *or* falsity (objective fact), us *or* them (ideology)—and as such brings the flow, the rhythm, the potential for attunement of existence to a halt. Sense, on the other hand, is the bodily-affective-orientating-significance that connects us, who or whatever us are, in the ongoing intertwining of relationality. As Nancy goes on to write, sense "is the relation as such, and nothing else"; it "is *that something like the transmission of a 'message' should be possible.*"[66] Sense is the possibility for communication as communing. This relational enchaining of sense, then, is simply another way of describing the *between* as the spacing of significance and concern.

Therefore, perhaps it is more productive to consider thinking giving way to sense rather than truth. Indeed, this is, I suggest, what Arendt is getting at when she argues that thinking becomes manifest as judgment. To be clear: one does not judge in the modality of thought or in the stepping-away of moral breakdown. One can judge anew only after having *returned* to the existential comfort of one's habituated modality of existence, that is, after having returned to the everyday modality of embodied morality. As Arendt put it, judgment is the manifestation of thought that gives us the "ability to tell right from wrong, beautiful from

---

62. O'Byrne 2015: 193.
63. For a collection of essays on carnal hermeneutics, see Kearney and Treanor 2015.
64. O'Byrne 2015: 194; italics added.
65. Nancy 1997: 14.
66. Nancy 1997: 118; italics in original.

ugly" amid the unthought of everydayness.[67] The capacity to judge anew after having thought, then, indicates a rebirth of sorts as one returns to the busyness and distractions of everyday life with a different—even if ever so slightly—embodied morality for being in the world comfortably with oneself and others.

Ethics and thinking end, then, with a return to the habituated embodied morality of everyday life; a return manifest in the capacity to judge with sense. Perhaps another way of saying this is that ethics and thinking allow one to return to their world with a sense of orientation, where orientation is a kind of understanding. Importantly, understanding is not meant here as a cognitive grasping by the brain. Rather, understanding is here intended existentially and etymologically as "standing in the midst of" the between of a world.[68] Understanding one's world, standing amidst a world, one can orientate oneself in an attuned manner such that one's world can make sense for now.

Thus, when Aleksandra Vladimirovna resolved to give her ticket money to the beggar, she was able to reorient herself in the world in a manner that made "good" sense to her and that she could understand. Or, after having spent so much time working at the chocolate café in the Downtown Eastside of Vancouver, Teresa was able to work through the various ethical demands she experienced as a drug user such that she regained an understanding of her world. Indeed, this new understanding and orientation in her world allowed Teresa to attune easily to the visiting anthropologist, who wasn't quite a friend but was far from a stranger. She understood her world, she could stand comfortably amidst her world, such that with a simple question—can I get you anything? Tranquilizers, aspirin, weed, acid, coke?—she brought about the "common" sense for us to spend our day together. In these ways and others, then, it is possible to say that understanding one's world, oneself, and those others there with one, things make sense, one has "good" sense, and the between us could be described in terms of a "common" sense.

All of this is to say that perhaps today truth is no longer (if it ever was) an appropriate concept for considering how it is between us. Perhaps instead, our worlds more than ever call us to think, and in so doing place a demand upon us to become ethical beings striving for a sense of worlds that are becoming increasingly complex. The question then might be: in these increasingly complex worlds of ours, how must we attune

---

67. Arendt 1978: 193.
68. See Zigon 2018, especially the epilogue.

such that it can be said that there is understanding between us? That is, how can we come to dwell trustingly in worlds of "common" sense?

These questions become even more difficult when power and inequality are considered, and the exclusion and oppression they oftentimes produce are exposed as seemingly insurmountable barriers to understanding and "common" sense. These questions, then, push beyond ethics. They reveal that ethics always implies a politics, and that the more complex the societal relationality, the more this ethico-politics calls for justice. The next chapter, then, will consider justice relationally.

CHAPTER 3

Justice (considered relationally)

In October of 2013, I was sitting in a packed auditorium in Denver, Colorado, at the opening ceremony of the largest gathering of anti-drug war activists on the globe. Among the audience that day, and participating in the conference that week, were representatives of drug user unions, drug policy organizations, and harm reduction and public health advocates from around the globe; a national organization of police chiefs and other law enforcement officials from around the globe who stand against the war on drugs; an organization of mothers whose children have died from overdoses and who now fight against the drug war; and a right-wing libertarian organization, among others. This audience, and those other participants at the conference, are indicative of a political movement that reflects the widely diffused complexity of the war on drugs against which it fights.[1]

It was here at this conference, among this odd mix of political activists, that I first began to realize that the war on drugs is indeed a widely diffused complex phenomenon, from which emerges a shared condition that affects the lives and ways of being of nearly everyone on the globe. That effect is, of course, differentially distributed situationally—for example, it affects a poor African-American male in the Bronx differently than it does a single White mother in Denmark, both of whom use

---

1. I use the terms "war on drugs" and "drug war" interchangeably as do most participants in the anti-drug war movement.

heroin; it affects a police chief in Seattle concerned with his budget and nonviolent policing differently than it does a parent who has lost a teen-age son to a prescription drug overdose—but yet this distribution re-mains within a range of possibilities set by the situations of the drug war, a shared condition that once recognized is obvious in its sharedness. There is no doubt that the sharedness of the drug war manifests differ-ently, for example, in Vancouver than it does in New York City, and in these differently than in Copenhagen or Denpasar or Moscow or Am-sterdam. But in each of these places and more, anti-drug war activists speak with certainty of a globally diffused phenomenon named the war on drugs that they are all equally caught up in.

At conferences such as this, or even in the everyday political activ-ity of local anti-drug war activists, where advocating for such things as policy change or establishing safe consumption rooms or any number of other necessary anti-drug war work is being done, it would be easy to miss that underlying all of this is an ethical demand for justice. This is precisely what Ethan Nadelmann, the executive director of the Drug Policy Alliance and likely the most visible spokesperson for the anti-drug war movement, tried to convey to the audience that day in the auditorium. For example, in the closing of his speech Nadelmann told the audience: "This is a long-term struggle for freedom; for freedom, for freedom and liberty. Yes, it's a passion for *justice* and science and health, but it is for freedom and for liberty [an audience member shouts out 'Yeah!']. Any one of us fighting against racism, fighting for more action for drug treatment, fighting for harm reduction, if you don't say those words 'freedom' and 'liberty,' and that's what this struggle is about every day, then you are selling short the values that we struggle for . . . the fight for ending the war on drugs."

In the previous chapter I explored the link between thinking and freedom. In this chapter, I expand on this by showing that sociopoliti-cally thinking and freedom manifest as justice. I do this by consider-ing justice relationally. Doing so is important because—as I argue—the contemporary condition is characterized by complex fragmentation and incoherence. And yet, increasingly this complexity is elided by a techno-data-centric worldview that attempts to render everything—including justice—predictable and calculable, in a word, algorithmic. A new and relational conception of justice is necessary to counter this tendency. To consider justice relationally, I will begin by exploring the assemblic na-ture of moralities and ethics, and then turn to how justice can be con-sidered in terms of the relational struggle to attune to these situated assemblages. Finally, I return to the anti-drug war movement to show how their very organization, as well as two of their primary concerns—policing and incarceration—can help us consider more specifically the necessity of thinking justice relationally.

Moral and Ethical Assemblages

Perhaps more than any other moral philosopher, Alasdair MacIntyre has influenced the trajectory of the anthropology of ethics.[2] This is not surprising considering that MacIntyre has been significantly influential in revitalizing the virtue ethics tradition, and many anthropologists have found this tradition helpful for addressing such anthropological concerns as embodiment, narrative, and social practice. Though these are certainly important for my own thinking, what I find most compelling about MacIntyre's work is his theoretical articulation of the fragmented and incoherent nature of ethics and justice in the contemporary condition.[3] Put simply, and not unlike the claims of post-truth, MacIntyre argues that there is no longer one coherent moral tradition upon which all (or most) people are compelled to engage in matters of ethical concern, dilemma, or crisis.

MacIntyre's diagnosis of modernity as a condition that lacks such a moral tradition for practical reasoning and claims of justice seems obviously correct. His course of treatment—as it were—for the revitalization of tradition as the basis for rational moral enquiry and debate is less obviously so. Perhaps one of the reasons for this is the slippage that is palpable in many of MacIntyre's books between the reasoning and debates of philosophers and that which occurs in everyday social life. If one focuses solely upon the former, it is difficult to find disagreement with MacIntyre. If, however, one is concerned with the question of how it is between us in everyday social lives, then one may be compelled to ask when and where was this life ever fully and completely shaped by one moral tradition?

Here is how MacIntyre characterizes contemporary late liberal persons in their everyday moral lives: "they tend to live *betwixt and between*, accepting usually unquestioningly the assumptions of the dominant

---

2. For just a few examples, see: Asad 2003; Mahmood 2005; Laidlaw 2014; Mattingly 2014.
3. MacIntyre 1981, 1988, 2016.

liberal individualist forms of public life, but drawing in different areas of their lives upon a variety of tradition-generated resources of thought and action, transmitted from a variety of familial, religious, educational, and other social and cultural sources."[4] I entirely agree—but with the caveat that this more or less accurately describes the moral experience of most persons at most times and places, minus, of course, the liberal individualist clause.[5] Most ordinary people have always had to negotiate the incoherencies and inconsistencies of everyday moral life, and their "success" in doing so goes a long way in answering the question of how it is between us.[6] That this negotiation, and these incoherencies and inconsistencies, are more obvious amid contemporary modernity than they might have been in the past or in contemporary smaller-scale societies, does not entail that they did not or do not exist in the latter two.[7] Rather, it may simply be the case that the global, social, and moral complexity of the contemporary condition makes it all but impossible to avoid.

Increasingly, ethnographic studies are emphasizing this complexity and the various ethical practices necessary for navigating it. Thus, for example, Sylvia Tidey has shown how Indonesian civil servants struggle to negotiate incoherencies and inconsistencies between local and familial obligations of care, international anti-corruption good governance regulations, and national attempts to adhere to the latter while acknowledging the import of the former.[8] As Merav Shohet has put it in her study of the moral life of Vietnamese families, the fact that what she calls moral lines are never clear-cut "underscore[s] aporia as an existential condition."[9] Although many of the ethnographies that have recently emphasized this have focused on social or historical moments of breakdown,[10] Shohet nevertheless emphasizes that aporia remains an existential condition "when life is at its most ordinary that drama and

---

4.   MacIntyre 1988: 397; italics added.

5.   See, for example, Zigon 2008, 2011.

6.   Just a few examples from so-called Western history: Brown 1989; Hadot 1995; Watts 2015; Wickham 2016.

7.   See, for example, the debate between Joel Robbins and me: Robbins 2004, 2007, 2009; Zigon 2009a, 2009b.

8.   Tidey 2022.

9.   Shohet 2021: 198.

10.   For example: Zigon 2010; Garcia 2010; Pinto 2014; Samuels 2019.

inconsistency characterize it."[11] Social and moral life just is characterized by incoherencies and inconsistencies.

This is so because in contrast to the internal coherence, consistency, and totality of a tradition, social worlds are best characterized in terms of a moral assemblage or constellation of incommensurable and oftentimes incompatible moral discourses and the diverse ethical practices that emerge from them. This moral fact, as it were, clearly emerged in my ethnographic research in post-Soviet Russia on morality and truth, which I briefly discussed in the previous chapter and which has been a clarifying theoretical-analytic in all my subsequent research. As such, I have elsewhere outlined a framework for thinking and articulating moral assemblages as a way for understanding the moral complexity of everyday social life.[12] Therefore, here I will only briefly summarize this concept.

The concept of moral assemblage helps us conceptualize what ethnographic analysis has made clear—that local and situated instances of ethical dilemma are often fraught with multiple conflicting and sometimes incommensurable moral motivations and possibilities.[13] Thus, for example, morality is frequently encountered in social worlds as various aspects of what I call: 1) *institutional morality*—for example, Catholic moral theology or international human rights doctrines; 2) *public discourses of morality*—for example, philosophical traditions such as MacIntyre hopes to revitalize or familial teachings or moral exemplars from literature; and 3) *embodied morality*—that unique dispositional way of being-with-others that each of us acquire over the course of our particular existential relational trajectory, and which I discussed in much detail in the two preceding chapters.

Therefore, what might come to *count* as morality within any situation is only constructed as a total and unified conception *after the fact*. For in the ongoing flow of the social world, that is, in the everyday intertwining of institutions, discourses, and persons, one only encounters *various aspects* of this moral assemblage. Put another way: no situation is predefined by one totalizing moral discursive tradition, and very few, if any, situations ever come to be defined by such after the fact. Rather, within

---

11.   Shohet 2021: 199.

12.   Zigon 2008, 2009a, 2011.

13.   See, for example: Zigon 2011, 2019; C. Scherz 2014; Hemment 2015; Bialecki 2017; Seale-Feldman 2020; Shohet 2021; Tidey 2022.

any given situation a unique localized moral assemblage emerges that is constituted by these various aspects.

Ethics, as I have been trying to articulate so far throughout this book, is a matter of ongoing attunement to these ever-emerging—and therefore, ever-shifting—situated moral assemblages. As if this were not difficult enough, a moral assemblage becomes even more complex when a second, and then a third person, each with their own unique embodied moralities, arrives. For the arrival of the second and the third with their unique embodied moralities alters the situated moral assemblage yet again, creating the demand for attunement once more. Upon their arrival, then, we move from an ethical situation to one of justice.

MacIntyre invokes Heraclitus's claim that justice is conflict to make the point that the "history of any society is thus in key part the history of an extended conflict or set of conflicts."[14] For MacIntyre, a tradition is an extended argument over time and is therefore characterized by internal conflict. Similarly, for MacIntyre the history of society is to a great extent a history of conflicting traditions. Again, this emphasis on the internal conflict of tradition and society is difficult to contest if one focuses solely upon such things as, for example, the history of philosophy or Christian theology, as MacIntyre mostly does. But in the everyday life of ordinary persons, the conflict of justice plays out along the differentiated and differentiating interstices of situated moral assemblages. If this is so, how then can justice be achieved? Is justice even possible?

Justice?

Today, justice is often considered in terms of fairness and distribution, in Rawlsian terms or otherwise. It is important to note, however, that justice as fairness and distribution is founded upon underlying assumptions of calculation and instrumentarianism. Justice, in this sense, gestures toward an algorithmic or recipe-like implementation. In contrast, Heraclitus's claim that justice is conflict—the claim that MacIntyre adopts—offers an alternative notion of justice as one of constant struggle. As struggle, justice is never realized but is always to come in the Derridean sense. That is, the struggle for justice—even in its "successes"—creates new opportunities for injustice, yet another conflict, and thus defers the very possibility of ever reaching the fulfillment and end of justice. The

---

14. MacIntyre 1988: 12.

very moment justice is "achieved," it slips away. In other words, the very struggle for justice entails the impossibility of justice. And yet, once the demand for justice is heard, one cannot avoid it. Some respond by ignoring the demand. But others become motivated and act for justice. Sometimes, perhaps, they even achieve justice momentarily but then it slips away with the sound of yet another demand that cannot be ignored. This is the frustration of justice: the demand for justice entails the impossibility of justice.

And yet, we respond; we must. Importantly, our response is not one of calculation, and neither is it one that follows a preestablished rule, principle, criteria, or grammar. To do so would be to confuse, as Derrida has pointed out, justice with law.[15] Rather, our response is one of attunement. In his essay-long interpretive-translation of Anaximander's fragment on justice, Heidegger at one point translates part of the fragment as "beings which linger awhile let belong, one to the other: consideration with regard to one another."[16] This is, one way of describing the attunement of justice that I am here trying to articulate. That Heidegger here intends by "beings" both human and nonhuman[17] is something to which I will return in the final chapter. For now, however, note that in his critical response to the essay, Derrida takes Heidegger to task for thinking *dikē*—the ancient Greek word often, and questionably so, translated as justice—as gathering, jointure, and the same.[18] Derrida, instead, wants to emphasize that the demand for justice arises precisely in the *dis*jointure. Justice must always remain out of joint, incalculable, and without the endpoint of totalization.

Derrida's reading of Heidegger on this point, however, may not be quite right. For Heidegger is articulating a *temporary* gathering that emerges out of and then withdraws again into disjointure. Thus, on my reading, Heidegger and Derrida are both attempting to articulate a notion of justice that matches well with my contention that, at the very least, justice is what we call the situated and temporary attempt to attune to the disparity and difference of contemporary and complex sociality in the form of moral assemblages. To respond to the demand for justice—to attune—is to "linger awhile" with others—that is, temporarily so—precisely because attunement is not a fusion into the same. Rather,

---

15. Derrida 1992a.
16. Heidegger 1975b: 46.
17. Heidegger 1975b: 40.
18. Derrida 1994: 23–28.

justice as attunement lets be(long) and allows one to linger awhile to consider the other as Other.

When we read Heidegger's interpretive-translation as such—and here it is again as a reminder: "beings which linger awhile let belong, one to the other: consideration with regard to one another"—we can see that justice need not be thought in terms of retribution or as a finalized order of totalized sameness (as other translations of Anaximander's fragment have been rendered, perhaps most famously by Nietzsche). But rather, justice could also be thought as a temporary attempt to be there situationally with others while also letting those others be. Such letting-be, it is important to note, does not entail dismissal, exclusion, contention, or violence, but rather consideration and care. The justice of letting-be is precisely what allows "us" to emerge while maintaining all our differences, rather than these differences being subsumed through exclusion and violence into a state of sharedness as sameness.

Such a notion of justice as attunement, then, is an offer of the gift of understanding. That is, understanding as I described it in the previous chapter, as a standing amidst the enigmatic differences of others and *not* as a grasping for sharedness as sameness. In this sense, we can think of justice in terms of attuning to—without eradicating—the constellation of differences that constitute our contemporary condition. And the demand for such a justice is perhaps most clearly experienced when we become caught up in the complexity of a situated moral assemblage.

Responding to the Demand for Justice—The Anti-Drug War Movement

Contemporary discourses tend to consider justice in terms of some standing in relation to a societal order or a law. Here again, though, we can invoke Derrida and his distinction between justice and law. Justice is distinct from law in that it is "the impulse, the drive, or the movement to improve the law, that is, to deconstruct the law."[19] Indeed, Derrida famously claimed that "deconstruction is a call for justice," precisely because it is justice that motivates the critical hermeneutic deconstruction of law that is a necessary "condition of historicity, revolution, morals,

---

19. Derrida 1997: 16; see also Derrida 1992a.

ethics, and progress."[20] In this sense, then, justice cannot be the calculative and algorithmic implementation of law. Rather, justice is the very condition for a critical response to an order of law that demands change because the latter is itself out of order, unattuned, or disjointed to the situation at hand. It is precisely such a notion of justice, I contend, that is taken up by many social movements today.

This is reminiscent of Sartre's articulation of justice as situationally adapting to the most marginalized—or as he put it, "the least favoured"[21]—and the complexity, ambiguity, and incompatible claims such an approach necessarily entails. Similarly, Iris Marion Young argues that our "conception of justice should begin with the concepts of domination and oppression."[22] Such a conception of justice acknowledges that the contemporary condition is socially constituted by both a constellation of differences between social groups and individuals, as well as the array of moral discourses, values, and concerns that is best understood in terms of a moral assemblage. Too often, however, the consequence of living in a contemporary condition of such constellations of difference and moral assemblages is that some groups and individuals are excluded, left out, dominated, and oppressed. Put another way, some are not counted as "us." The demand to address this exclusion, domination, and oppression is the demand for justice. Note, however, that the eradication of difference, or what could also be called assimilation, should *not* be the aim of justice. Rather, justice ought to give way to "social relations of difference without exclusion," of which, Young contends, city life—in its ideal form—offers us an example.[23]

In this sense, the most contemporary of social movements today is what I call the anti-drug war movement, with which I have done extensive ethnographic fieldwork. What do I mean by saying that it is the most contemporary? Certainly, this movement is an exemplar of a justice movement of the sort Young likely would have endorsed: a movement that seeks to overcome domination and oppression by creating "social relations of difference without exclusion." But its contemporaneity goes well beyond this. For, if the contemporary condition—as noted at the end of the previous section—is characterized by an increasingly complex constellation of differences and moral assemblages, then, as I argued

---

20. Derrida 1997: 16.
21. Sartre 1968.
22. Young 1990: 3.
23. Young 1990: 227.

in *A War on People*, social movements of the twenty-first century must organize in a manner that reflects this assemblic complexity. As the political theorist William Connolly argues, any social movement adequate to the contemporary condition must be constituted as what he calls a "radical, pluralist assemblage."[24] As he goes on to describe it, such a social movement would be anchored

> entirely in no single class, gender, ethnic group, creed, or generation, the formation of such a vital pluralist assemblage involves moving back and forth between the micropolitics of media life and local involvements, the internal ventilation of the faith constituencies to which we belong, the confrontation of corporate leaders, active investments in electoral politics, and participation in cross-state citizen movements.[25]

To which I would add, an adequate reflection of the moral assemblage that has emerged around the situation being addressed, in my case here, the war on drugs.

The anti-drug war movement is precisely such a pluralist assemblage of diverse, and sometimes seemingly contradictory, groups and organizations that have created a counter-hegemonic alternative to what I have described as the global condition of war as governance.[26] For example, the global anti-drug war movement consists of, among others, unions of active drug users (primarily users of heroin and crack cocaine, but also groups of marijuana users) and their most immediate allies such as drug policy organizations, harm reduction advocates, and housing reform organizations. Importantly, though, this global movement also consists of such unexpected participants as organizations of law enforcement against the drug war, right-wing libertarians, and the parents of those who have died drug war deaths. Many of these unions, groups, and organizations have become globally networked, regularly meet to share

---

24. Connolly 2013: 137.
25. Connolly 2013: 137.
26. For my take on war as governance, see Zigon 2019. For the need to build an ecology of organizations and provide a counter-hegemonic alternative, see Srnicek and Williams 2015: chapters 7 and 8. For the now classic post-Marxian articulation of hegemony and counter-hegemony, see Laclau and Mouffe 2001.

ideas and experiences, and have come to agree on a long-term strategy for ending the war on drugs.

To say that the anti-drug war movement is globally networked is not hyperbole. For these unions, groups, and organizations that constitute the movement exist in nearly every country. Yet, because each of these unions, groups, and organizations are characterized by their own singular localized moral assemblage—constituted by diverse aspects of localized institutional, public discursive, and embodied moralities—they bring these to the global movement, which then reconstitutes them as yet another moral assemblage of the diverse participants.

The assemblic nature of the anti-drug war movement is necessary because the war on drugs itself is best considered as a widely diffused and complex assemblage. Having roots in the nineteenth century and gradually emerging throughout the twentieth, the war on drugs was officially "declared" in 1971 by Richard Nixon and only became a full-blown global war in the 1980s, when it became militarized and intertwined with the Cold War through initiatives of the Reagan and George H. W. Bush administrations. Today what is named the war on drugs is responsible for hundreds of thousands of deaths a year globally, and the social and political "death" or exclusion of many more.[27]

Importantly, the war on drugs must be understood as more than simply drug laws and policy. For today it has become so widely diffused and complexly intertwined with much of everyday life, that in one way or another it affects nearly everyone. Thus, whether by means of military interventions, policing and incarceration strategies, international and national surveillance, and the overblown budgets to pay for them—or by means of biopolitical therapeutics, national and international legislation, and the normalization of labor regimes and discipline—or by means of the recursive affects and (re)creation of inequalities of race, ethnicity, gender, and class, all of which and more constitute aspects of the war on drugs—this is a war that potentially affects every human on the planet. This is why when I write that the anti-drug war movement is perhaps the most contemporary of all social movements, I mean this not only in its organizational sense but, above all, in its wide-reaching consequences. In a very real way, our social futures depend upon this movement's success.

Despite the global reach of this political movement, much of their activity is done at the local or regional levels, addressing what I call the localized situations of the more widely diffused complexity of the war on

---

27. See UNDOC 2014: 3; Drug Policy Alliance, http://www.drugpolicy.org.

drugs. Still, because these localized situations are manifestations of the globally diffused complexity of the war on drugs, these political agonists find themselves in a shared condition of war that is more or less the same no matter where it manifests. As a result, although tactics and strategies differ to some extent according to the differences of the situated manifestations—policing and incarceration in the United States are much more oppressive and violent than, for example, in Denmark or Canada—overall the global anti-drug war movement has been able to construct a coherent long-term strategy because they have been able to recognize that they are all, in fact, caught up in shared conditions despite the local differences.

Each of these groups brings to the movement their own unique constellation of moral discourses and motivations that inform their ethical and political activity, the combination of which constitute the moral assemblage of the anti-drug war movement. In over a decade's time of research, I regularly heard invocations of such diverse moral discourses and motivations as: libertarian and, not dissimilarly, anarchist conceptions of freedom; demands for dignity that have their foundation in either various theological traditions or the human rights tradition or a combination thereof; claims of rights that have their reference point as either the human rights tradition or nation-state-based civil, social, or political rights as enshrined in constitutions or laws; and, petitions for care based in public health or biomedical or psychosocial therapeutics but always with the underlying assumption that care, above all, is what we are obliged to offer other human beings.

The anti-drug war movement, then, is a pluralist assemblage that— in addition to being a successful social movement—must negotiate this constellation of diverse and at times contradictory moral discourses and motivations to allow a "common" sense to emerge within the movement. This negotiation is often done by those in the movement by means of what Shohet calls sideshadowing, a narrative tactic for entertaining a multiplicity of moral "perspectives, possibilities, and temporalities."[28] Indeed, as Shohet goes on to explain, sideshadowing is precisely a narrative tactic for navigating the oftentimes contradictory and incommensurate nature of moral assemblages.[29] Thus, the movement's success is above all incumbent upon the realization of this "common" sense—even if only temporarily but regularly realized—for without it, no collective ethical or political activity is possible.

---

28. Shohet 2021: 18.
29. Shohet 2021: 188.

I have written extensively about the anti-drug war movement elsewhere, so I do not want to rehearse it here any further. For our purposes, I simply hope to point out that it is an example of how social movements in the twenty-first century must organize and act in order to have success. It seems that gradually this is the case as, for example, Black Lives Matter or the climate change movement are increasingly taking on this assemblic nature. For in addition to addressing the obvious issues of the war on drugs—drug policy, the spread of infectious disease, punitive policing, mass incarceration, stigma, housing and labor restrictions related to drug use, overdose—the globally-networked anti-drug war movement is at the forefront of offering an alternative political and social imaginary to our contemporary condition that would benefit everyone. In particular, this anti-drug war imaginary and political activity is enacting non-normative, open, and relationally inclusive alternatives such as a community of whoever arrives; freedom that lets others be to become what and who they will; and care as attuned to the singular need of the other.

The result is a politics of action that has lasting and sustainable outcomes. Consequently, this politics of worldbuilding has been able to go beyond momentary prefiguration, spectacle, and protest, which has come to characterize much left-leaning political activity of the last generation or so. Like Havel's "existential revolution," this form of politics is building new worlds that include not only its infrastructure, values, and social and worldly interactive practices, but the onto-ethical grounds for such worlds. Indeed, the alternative worlds this movement is helping bring about can offer guidance in rethinking some of today's most basic political and ethical motivations, tactics, and aims. That is, to a rethinking of the very idea and practice of justice.

Algorithmic "Justice"

Recall that for Derrida justice is not the calculative and algorithmic implementation of law. Rather, justice is the very condition for a critical response to an order of law that demands change because the latter is itself out of order. As such, justice is the "condition of historicity, revolution, morals, ethics, and progress" because it motivates a critical hermeneutic deconstruction of law that is (or has become) out of order, or unattuned to situations.[30] It is with this understanding of justice that

---

30. Derrida 1997: 16.

one of the anti-drug war movement's central concerns—policing and mass incarceration—is best understood as a concern for justice. For since the 1980s—and this is especially so in the United States—law in relation to drug use has become increasingly calculative and algorithmic. This is best understood by considering two aspects of policing and mass incarceration—Stop-and-Frisk and mandatory minimums—and their most recent incarnations—data-driven predictive policing and recidivism programs. Indeed, in ways that in retrospect seem obvious, policing in the United States has been at the forefront of what today could be called our data-centric society and the surveillance and lack of privacy this entails, to which I will turn in the next chapter.

Stop-and-Frisk is a policing policy first implemented in New York City under the administration of Mayor Michael Bloomberg. Though as of 2013 it has been ruled to be unconstitutional in the United States, Stop-and-Frisk and similar police tactics are likely the most "successful" of the war on drugs across the globe. Stop-and-Frisk essentially means that police officers with so-called reasonable suspicion can stop any individual to question and frisk him. This tactic that initially aimed at getting weapons off the streets eventually morphed into a means of controlling and watching populations. And no segment of the population in the United States is controlled and watched more by this and similar forms of surveillance than Black and Brown persons, and primarily young men.[31]

In 2012, for example, over 500,000 individuals were stopped and frisked in New York City alone, 87 percent of whom were either Black or Brown. Perhaps most disturbing about this form of surveillance is that 89 percent of these stops turned up nothing. Yet, the highest number of those arrested (over 5000) were arrested for possessing personal-use quantities of marijuana, which under New York City law is not an offence unless the marijuana is shown in public, which it is when a police officer asks you to empty your pockets. Overwhelmingly those stopped, frisked, and arrested are young Black and Brown men, and this tactic is predominantly carried out in the neighborhoods where these men live.[32] The result is that this very real possibility of Stop-and-Frisk that many

---

31. M. Alexander 2012: 63–71.
32. For this and other information see: http://www.nyclu.org/content/stop-and-frisk-data and http://www.nyclu.org/news/analysis-finds-racial-disparities-ineffectiveness-nypd-stop-and-frisk-program-links-tactic-soar. Both accessed on July 29, 2023.

Black and Brown men must live with every day in New York and else-where, has left many feeling that their neighborhood, their street, and even their own front stoop is no longer a place where they can dwell.[33]

Consider, for example, the experience of Terrance. During my ethno-graphic research in New York, I came to know Terrance quite well. As a fifty-year-old Black man from the Bronx, a former crack user who has been incarcerated twice, and now a leader of VOCAL—likely the most important anti-drug war organization in the country—Terrance had a lot to say about his experiences with police. For example, once he told me: Stop-and-Frisk tactics make him feel as if "I'm trespassing in my own neighborhood." He continued with a description of his experience with Stop-and-Frisk:

> If I'm coming out of my building, like I been many times, and stopped and frisked because I'm a person of color and I don't have my sneak-ers tied or I'm wearing, you know, or I have clothes on that are related to gangsters or whatever, which are the clothings that a lot of people in the neighborhood wear, you know, and I'm going to work and I'm still being stopped. And I got my bag and everything, my ID is out, you know, come on. You're not giving me no freedom to walk in my own neighborhood, but if I was in another neighborhood, another color, you wouldn't be stopping me. So why am I, at this point right here, being profiled?

Terrance's experience and the question it poses for him discloses a cen-tral aspect of the Stop-and-Frisk policy—it is an attempt to implement algorithmic "justice."

In contrast to justice as attunement that I have been trying to de-scribe so far in this chapter, the contemporary condition is perhaps best characterized as only offering what I will call, in quotes, "justice," which is the imposition of law or policy without thought in relation to situa-tions. Here it is important to introduce the concept of the algorithm: "an algorithm is a recipe, an instruction set, a sequence of tasks to achieve a particular calculation or result."[34] In this sense, "justice" is already semi-algorithmic in that the absence of thought in relation to situations al-ready entails the imposition of law or policy as a consequence of some

---

33. For an ethnographic description of this in Philadelphia, see Goffman 2014.

34. Finn 2017: 17.

prejudice—some prejudgment—of how or upon whom such law or policy ought to be imposed. Thus, when Stop-and-Frisk policy results in the stopping, frisking, and questioning of over 400,000 Black and Brown (mostly) young men in one year in one city, it seems rather clear that justice is not being done but "justice" most certainly is.

Although Stop-and-Frisk is clearly a matter of "justice," it is not yet the full realization of algorithmic "justice." For although Stop-and-Frisk policy was and remains one founded upon systemic racism, there always remains the possibility that in any situation the implementation of the policy will not be carried out by a particular police officer. The existence of this possibility—no matter how slight it may be—indicates the nonexistence of the fully functional algorithm. For the fully functional algorithm entails that there remains no possibility of possibility. Put another way, the fully functional algorithm eliminates any possibility of thought whatsoever. Without thought there can be neither judgment nor possibility. Understood as such, justice implemented algorithmically is an impossibility. Algorithmic "justice," on the other hand, is increasingly the norm.

Consider the increasing use by local police departments of predictive policing programs. Utilizing historical crime data, these predictive policing programs calculate—and continuously recalculate—where the next crime is likely to occur. Such programs are extremely helpful to local police departments, and especially those of small cities that increasingly face budget concerns. Using these predictive policing programs, departments can now deploy officers at certain times and in particular locations oftentimes the size of just a couple of football fields. The consequence—at least in some cases—is a significant drop in some crimes.[35]

Importantly, predictive policing programs utilize historical crime data to predict time and location of future crimes. Note, however, that this data is often the result of policing policy and tactics that for over a generation (if not longer) have focused primarily on lower-income neighborhoods, and especially those of persons of color. Furthermore, because of these policies and tactics, the data is overwhelmingly constituted by rather low-level crimes such as possession of personal-use amounts of drugs or unlicensed street vending. Consequently, the predictions these programs make will focus future policing on poor people, often Black and Brown, committing mostly low-level crimes.

---

35. O'Neil 2016: 85.

For example, for decades Stop-and-Frisk and similar policies were largely carried out in neighborhoods of Black and Brown working-class people. Although this surveillance and harassment rarely turned up anything illegal, occasionally it did, and this would become part of the historical crime data. What was normally discovered in such encounters was rather petty—personal-use amounts of marijuana, underage drinking, occasionally an unregistered gun—as well as relatively low-level crimes discovered simply because the police were already there—unlicensed street vending, car break-ins, loitering. The fact that many of these crimes also happen in more affluent and predominantly White neighborhoods—as well as other kinds of crimes like tax evasion or insider trading—never becomes part of the historical crime data because the police are not policing these neighborhoods.

It is precisely this already biased crime data that is the foundation for predictive policing programs, which lead to more policing of already overpoliced neighborhoods, which results in the accumulation of more data that says that crime is done in these neighborhoods, and the feedback simply reinforces the future prediction.[36] Predictive policing programs, then, are best understood as the implementation of algorithmic "justice." Such programs eliminate the need of police departments and officers to think and make judgments. Rather, they simply need to follow the algorithmic recipe for fighting crime. Consequently, there is no longer any possibility that thought in relation to a situation could occur and, thus, that some officer might make the judgment that this here and now is not worthy of attention. Because the predictions these algorithms provide are simply repetitions of historical data—data, that is, which is fundamentally biased and limited—they will result in little more than the repetition of past injustices. The difference now is that the algorithm offers no possibility for the possibility of acting otherwise. Algorithmic "justice," then, entails the repetition of past injustices without the possibility of change.

Stop-and-Frisk and similar police tactics are likely the most "successful" ones in the war on drugs, and predictive policing programs have now made these tactics even more calculative and algorithmic. They are responsible not only for a significant amount of the surveillance the drug war allows to be placed on neighborhoods and individuals, but also contribute to the vast increase of incarceration rates in the United States and other countries, and particularly for the incarceration of those carrying

---

36.   Benjamin 2019: chapter 2.

small, personal use amounts of marijuana. Indeed, the policing and surveillance techniques of the war on drugs are largely responsible for the mass incarceration of nonviolent and low-level drug users around the globe, as the global prison population has skyrocketed in the last three decades to over 11 million persons.[37]

But no country incarcerates drug users, and its population in general, like the United States, which now has the highest level of incarceration on the planet. In fact, the United States has the highest level of incarceration in modern history approached, but not surpassed, only by the Soviet gulag system under Stalin.[38] The war on drugs and its often racialized tactics have fed this mass incarceration, such that, for example, in 2020 1.16 million people were arrested on nonviolent drug charges, the vast majority of whom were Black and Brown.[39] Indeed, those who profit from this carceral political-economics recognize the centrality of current drug policy and laws to their corporate success. For example, in a 2010 report to the United States Securities and Exchange Commission, the country's "largest owner and operator of privatized correctional and detention facilities" highlighted changes to current drug law as one of the primary risks to its growth and profit.[40] This recognition and concern is not surprising; since 1980 the prison population in the United States has increased by 500 percent, and Stop-and-Frisk and other forms of drug war surveillance have been key factors in these skyrocketing numbers. Thus, for example, in 1980, a total of 41,000 drug offenders were in all state and federal prisons and local jails, while in 2023 this total stood at 353,000.[41]

If Stop-and-Frisk and now increasingly predictive policing programs allow for the surveillance and apprehension of populations at extraordinary rates, then mandatory minimum sentencing has been responsible for putting these populations in the prisons once they are swept up.

---

37. https://www.prisonstudies.org/ (accessed July 29, 2023). See also: M. Alexander 2012; Dilts 2014: 9; Goffman 2014: xii, 3; Hari 2015: 93–96, 109–10.
38. Goffman 2014: xiii.
39. These statistics come from the Drug Policy Alliance website unless otherwise noted. See http://www.drugpolicy.org (accessed July 29, 2023).
40. Corrections Corporation of America, "2010 Annual Report on Form 10-K." Annual Report Pursuant to Section 13 or 15(d) of the Securities Exchange Act of 1934, December 31, 2010: 2, 19.
41. See https://www.prisonpolicy.org (accessed July 29, 2023).

Federal mandatory minimum sentencing has been used in the United States since the 1980s and it is overwhelmingly used in cases of non-violent, low-level, minor drug offenses.[42] Typically, a first-time offender will receive five or ten years in prison.[43] Some first-time offenders have received life in prison.[44] Again, it is important to emphasize that these offenders are not cartel members or bigtime dangerous dealers—they are overwhelmingly ordinary people who got caught with personal use amounts of drugs or similar minor offenses.

Importantly, prosecutors often use these heavy-handed mandatory minimums as a way to avoid trial and pressure an accused person to plea bargain. Indeed, this is one of the primary ways in which prosecutors can "turn" people to "snitch" on others. Given the choice of ten years in prison for a minor drug offense or "ratting" someone out in exchange for a reduced sentence, many choose the latter option. Too often, this choice is taken even by those who are innocent of the crime they are charged with. The result is that it is estimated that two to five percent of the US prison population is innocent of what they were charged—this is tens of thousands of persons.[45] Perhaps more than any other policing and incarceration policy, mandatory minimum sentencing is responsible for mass incarceration in the United States. And this is so because it is a perfect example of algorithmic "justice."

As already noted, fully functional algorithmic "justice" is the erasure of possibility, the erasure of hope. This is so because its imposition is thoughtless in relation to its pertinent situation. Put another way: algorithmic "justice" forecloses attunement, and without thoughtful attunement there is neither judgment nor possibility. All of this perfectly describes mandatory minimum sentencing. Because the sentencing is already prescribed prior to any particular commitment of the crime, the situational particularities of the crime are not considered. Was the person living in poverty, physically abused her entire life, and addicted to heroin for ten years? No matter! The sentence is already mandatorily prescribed. Did the person unknowingly drive a friend to a minor drug deal? No matter! The sentence is already mandatorily prescribed. Did one's son hide a small amount of crack in your house unbeknownst to you? No matter! The sentence is already mandatorily prescribed, and you

---

42. M. Alexander 2012: 92.
43. M. Alexander 2012: 87.
44. M. Alexander 2012: 90.
45. M. Alexander 2012: 87–89.

will now spend at least ten years in prison. Judges in these cases are simply not allowed to judge. Consequently, the defendants in these cases are left hopeless and without possibility. Or, as Supreme Court Justice Anthony Kennedy has put it: "In all too many cases, mandatory minimum sentences are unjust."[46]

Increasingly, there is talk of criminal justice reform in the United States and mandatory minimum sentencing is often a central aspect of it. Certainly, eliminating mandatory minimums would be just. Recall, however, that the very moment justice is "achieved" it slips away. One responds to the demand for justice by becoming motivated and acting to achieve that which is demanded. When achieved, it is so only momentarily; it then slips away with the call of yet another demand that cannot be avoided. This is the frustration of justice: the demand of justice entails the impossibility of justice. And so it is with criminal justice reform. For even if, someday, mandatory minimum sentencing is eliminated, its replacement is likely already in place—recidivism models—which seem poised to be even more unjust than mandatory minimums.

Recidivism models are based on in-depth questionnaires given to persons who have been convicted of a crime or are already incarcerated. Their responses are the basis for each of them being categorized as high, medium, or low risk for recidivism. Though meant to address the issue of recidivism, parole, and possible anti-recidivism programs, increasingly some states are using these models as a guide for sentencing. As Cathy O'Neil rightly and bluntly puts it: this is unjust.[47]

Recidivism models may present themselves as a more just process to guide sentencing, but the centrality of personal data to these models—and the black box that renders these models opaque to the average person—entails that increasingly it appears that individuals are sentenced not simply for what they did but for *who they are*.[48] For as unjust as mandatory minimum sentencing is, at least in theory it does not matter if one is White, Black, poor, rich, or whatever: if you are convicted of the crime you do the time. In theory. But with so-called recidivism models, the time to be done seems to be based largely on one's existential trajectory, that is, who one is. For the models—such as the LSI-R model, which is one of the most used—not only ask questions about previous

---

46. M. Alexander 2012: 93.
47. O'Neil 2016: 26.
48. O'Neil 2016: 26.

convictions, but also about the "circumstances of [one's] birth and up-bringing, including his or her family, neighborhood, and friends."[49]

As we already know from such policing tactics as Stop-and-Frisk, certain neighborhoods—often those predominantly populated by Black and Brown persons—are significantly more policed than others. The result of this is that if one lives in such a neighborhood, then one is much more likely to have had previous encounters with police, and so have one's friends and family. Since these neighborhoods are poorer than those that are not policed heavily, it is also more likely that all these people at some point would have been or were currently unemployed at the time of arrest. Answering positively to questions related to these circumstances likely puts one in the "high risk" category (though the black box of the models makes it very difficult to know for sure), and thus to receive a longer sentence or be denied parole.

Furthermore, since these neighborhoods are also predominantly those of Black and Brown people, the recidivism models do not need to ask specifically about race—which is illegal to do anyway—because the answer to that question is already historically "baked in" to the answers to many of the other questions. As Ruha Benjamin has put it, the black box of algorithms is often, in effect, an anti-Black box.[50] Consequently, those who fall into the "high risk" category are much more likely to be people of color. And thus, the algorithmic "justice" imposed by recidivism models seems likely to enact systemic racism even more perniciously than mandatory minimums.

The demand for justice in relation to criminal justice is loud. The anti-drug war movement that I discussed in the previous section is responding to this demand, as are others. But caution is necessary. The promise often made by Big Data is that more data and better algorithms will help bring about a better world. This promise, however, is increasingly exposed as illusion, or perhaps, delusion. And yet, Big Data seems unstoppable as its other promises of profit, budget savings, and efficiency are all being fulfilled. The bottom line is once again trumping ethics and a more just world. Predictive policing programs and recidivism models—like many "solutions" offered by Big Data—cloak themselves in ethics and justice but are better understood in terms of budgetary bottom lines and efficiency, often with systemic racism baked in. And while they may save states and taxpayers some money, they are enacting a form

---

49. O'Neil 2016: 26.
50. Benjamin 2019.

of algorithmic "justice" that is potentially far more pernicious than any injustice we have yet to know. This is so because the algorithmic "justice" offered by Big Data only offers the infinite repetition of past injustice. Consequently, such algorithmic "justice" will remain forever thoughtless, eradicating all possibility for judgment, and thus closing any opening to an otherwise. As such, the algorithmic "justice" of Big Data will leave us with unjust worlds shaped by the unstoppable cold consequence of calculative repetition.[51]

Some Final Words

I have been considering justice relationally. Beginning with the demand for justice made by the global anti-drug war movement, I showed that understanding the contemporary condition in terms of moral and ethical assemblages helps us see the necessity of assemblic social movements today, and that the thoughtlessness of algorithmic "justice" will increasingly be one of their primary concerns. In doing so, I showed that the response to the demand for justice is best considered in terms of attunement. Our response to this demand—our acting justly—must be, I have argued, attuning to—without eradicating—the constellation of differences that constitute the contemporary condition. Once the third arrives and we have moved beyond ethics to the political, then any justice that does not ultimately descend into the thoughtlessness of an algorithm can be nothing other than the constant struggle to keep attuning. There may be temporary moments of lingering together in consideration and care but one thing that history tells us is certain, a new demand for justice will soon arrive. When it does, we must, once again, respond.

---

51. See Caputo 1997: 137.

CHAPTER 4

What is Data (Ethics)?

The previous chapter made clear that we have now entered what the bioethicist Paul Scherz calls the age of algorithmic governance.[1] With this new form of governance, ethics has become a concern. There are good reasons for this. For example, worries about data privacy or data-driven surveillance, or the increased intertwining of the data industry with the finance industry or the so-called defense industry. The fact that data-extracting and data-driven algorithms increasingly regulate the temporal, affective, and intersubjective modalities of everyday life. And the sometimes over-the-top, but sometimes legitimate, concerns of how artificial intelligence may change the very definition of the human, as well as life itself. Indeed, all of this makes the increasing dominance of data-centric technologies in everyday life both an ethical and existential concern. There are good reasons, then, for why we are experiencing an ethical demand made by the data-centric situation in which we now find ourselves.

What is too often missing from this demand, however, is the very question of the ethics appropriate to data. This is so, because we have neglected to ask the even more fundamental question: what is data? For it is precisely our response to this more fundamental question that leads us to our ethical starting point. This is so because any ethics begins with ontological assumptions about what loosely can be called the "subject,"

---

1. P. Scherz 2022.

"object," and "processes" of ethics. And the question of data is fundamentally an ontological question. Therefore, if we are to ask the question of data ethics, we must begin by questioning the ontology of data.

This chapter unfolds as a query. First, I ask how data is conceived by what I call the data-centric industry and its practitioners, and sketch one version of the so-called ethical response to this conception of data, that is, the call for the right to data privacy. What I hope to show is that the so-called ethical response of privacy is not ethics but rather economics masquerading as ethics. This is so in large part because of the ontological assumptions of the data-centric industry, assumptions which are too often shared by those who critique it. As a response to this, I ask how shifting the way in which we conceive of data might allow for an appropriate (and actual) ethical response. Invoking the Latin origin of data—*datum*: something given as gift—I draw from Jean-Luc Marion's phenomenology of the given to continue my articulation of relational ethics as one well suited for addressing many of our contemporary ethical problems. Indeed, as I have been arguing so far in this book, relational ethics is not only more appropriate to these contemporary challenges, but more appropriate to the very idea of ethics as such. That is, to ethics as an ongoing process of relational attunement, the political manifestation of which is justice.

Data as Information-Fact

What is data? A recent introductory text to data science defines data as a "piece of information" or as "an abstraction (or measurement) from a real-world entity (person, object, or event)."[2] This concise definition is revealing. It tells us much about the basic assumptions of the data-centric worldview. First, as pieces of information, data are facts about something or someone collected by various means of investigation. Second, these information-facts, as I will call them, are not to be confused with those things or persons as they are in the "real world" but are, instead, abstractions or measurements. As the authors of this text put it:

> Data are generated through a process of abstraction, so any data are the result of human decisions and choices. For every abstraction, somebody (or some set of people) will have made choices with regard

---

2.   Kelleher and Tierney 2018: 39, 240.

to what to abstract from and what categories or measurements to use in the abstracted representation. The implication is that data are never an objective description of the world. They are instead always partial and biased.[3]

In other words, data as information-facts are interpretations.

Despite the recognition of this, it seems clear that the data-centric worldview elides this crucial aspect of what data is, and instead considers these information-facts as representative of—or a mirror of—the real-world entities from which they were abstracted. Indeed, the very notion of "real-world entities" carries with it a strong sense that these entities exist objectively—out there—in the real world; and although we may not be capable of coming to know them in their objective realness, if our methods are good enough, then our representations will be as good as objective knowledge.

As the authors go on to say, "the data we use for data science are not a perfect representation of the real-world entities and processes we are trying to understand, but if we are careful in how we design and gather the data that we use, then the results of our analysis will provide useful insights into our real-world problems."[4] Data may be interpretation, the thinking seems to go, but with the proper design and methods our interpretations can legitimately be *considered to be* (glossed as "useful insights") objective facts in the "real world." I suggest it is this key move of the *considered to be* that collapses the distinction between objectivity and interpretation that is too often forgotten in data-centric practices.

Thus, we can make a claim starting from which we will continue our argument in the rest of this chapter: for most data-centric corporations, institutions, and practitioners—or what I call the data-centric industry—data are considered as observable, extractable, categorizable, and indexable facts in the world. These objective facts are conceived as out there, sitting dormant, filled with potential, ready to release their hidden value once properly collected and instrumentalized. Indeed, the very terms used in the data-centric industry to describe its own processes are indicative of this conception of data. Like coal and oil, data is yet another "raw material" to be (data-) mined, extracted, rendered (analyzed), and sold.

---

3. Kelleher and Tierney 2018: 46.
4. Kelleher and Tierney 2018: 46–47.

For a long time, global capitalism has considered raw material and natural resources as a part of nature, over which humans claim power and right to dominate and manipulate toward their own ends. Data as raw material is conceived similarly but with the caveat that it transcends the nature/culture dichotomy. As such, data is considered to be everywhere: from the atmosphere to a traffic intersection to mortgage lending. Most disconcertingly, however, data as raw material is to be discovered in and extracted from our phones, homes, cars, bodies, and affective lives, along with nearly everything else one could name that is a part of who we are and how we live our everyday lives. Put another way, human experience has become the primary raw material for the data-centric industries. We and our lives have become to the data-centric industry little more than what a coalfield is to the mining industry: a source to be mined. Just as the forests, mountains, and rivers have for a very long time been ontologically rendered as standing reserve,[5] in place for little more than human use, today everything—and most especially human experience itself—has been ontologically rendered standing reserve in place for the profit of a few. Recall that according to the authors of the introductory data science text I quoted from above, not only do well-designed data practices result in insights into the real world, but *useful* insights. The contemporary ontological condition, then, may best be articulated in the following manner: to be is to be of useful-value. Note that by useful-value I intend at one and the same time to gesture toward the use-value of Marxian economics and to indicate the way data is always available for multiple potential uses: useful, that is, as always already full of potential but as of yet unknown uses.

This extraction imperative is now central to what Shoshana Zuboff calls surveillance capitalism. This new form of capitalism—the ground for which was laid by neoliberal policies of deregulation—Zuboff defines as the unilateral claim of "human experience as free raw material for translation into behavioral data."[6] She goes on to describe what happens next:

Although some of these data are applied to product or service improvement, the rest are declared as a proprietary *behavioral surplus*, fed into advanced manufacturing processes known as "machine intelligence," and fabricated into *prediction products* that anticipate what

5. Heidegger 1977.
6. Zuboff 2019: 8.

you will do now, soon, and later. Finally, these prediction products are traded in a new kind of marketplace for behavioral predictions that [Zuboff calls] *behavioral futures markets*. Surveillance capitalists have grown immensely wealthy from these trading operations, for many companies are eager to lay bets on our future behavior.[7]

Importantly, we are not the customers in this new paradigm of surveillance capitalism, but rather the products. Or perhaps it is better to say: we are both resource and product linked through a disciplinary recursive loop whereby our words, actions, and affective lives are mirrored back to us in a fabricated manner so as to nudge us to take a particular predetermined action. Every time you are suddenly inundated by online advertisements for new mattresses, for example, after recently talking with someone about your lower back pain or simply searching online for exercises to strengthen and stretch your back, you have just experienced surveillance capitalism as both resource and product. The customer, in this case, is the advertising agencies and the mattress companies that have paid for access to this behavioral data in expectation of profit. These profits, however, only come when we—as product—act in a way to bring them about, that is, when we purchase the mattress.

The question, however, is: did we buy the mattress because we wanted to or as the result of automated behavior modification recursively enacted upon us? Perhaps we will never know. But one thing we know for certain is that surveillance capitalism's *modus operandi* is to alter our behavior to act in ways that result in massive amounts of profit for those who know how to do so. As one chief data scientist in Silicon Valley told Zuboff: "The goal of everything we do is to change people's actual behavior at scale. We want to figure out the construction of changing a person's behavior, and then we want to change how lots of people are making their day-to-day decisions."[8] The aim of this, as he went on to tell Zuboff, is to come to know "how profitable certain behaviors are for us." The shaping of our actions—indeed, the shaping of who we are—by surveillance capitalism, Zuboff claims, is a new form of power she calls instrumentarianism. This is a form of power that "knows and shapes human behavior toward others' ends."[9] Whether we call this instrumentarian

---

7. Zuboff 2019: 8; italics in original.
8. Zuboff 2019: 297.
9. Zuboff 2019: 8.

power, or following Deleuze[10] call it control, or following Heidegger[11] call it Enframing, the point is that in a data-driven technological world, it is increasingly impossible to escape conditions that render the human little more than a standing reserve for the manipulation and profit of an elite few.

What we see, then, is that the elision of the interpretive aspect of data—what we can call the original elisionary sin of data-centric practice—renders data little more than information-facts that are said to objectively represent the real world. This, in turn, leads to such data being utilized to feed back into and alter these "real-world entities" for profit. To be even more precise, there is a double elision done by the data-centric industry in that not only does it forget its own interpretive processes, but in doing so it covers over the very hermeneutic nature of its primary raw material—that is, human experience—rendering this experience as behavior.[12] Consequently, this double elision turns the essential hermeneutic nature of human experience into the illusory objectivity of behavior, which far from being "real" is merely a projection of the designs, methods, and practices of the data-centric industry.

The Right to Privacy

Increasingly, this situation is recognized as problematic, and calls for protective measures are being made. The right to data privacy is a growing consensus in response to the new ethical imperative to "protect our data!" Whether conceived and articulated in more traditional liberal terms of individual privacy or in post-liberal terms as, for example, dividual privacy,[13] the assumption seems to be that only a defense of privacy can protect us and our data. It is important to note, however, that several assumptions are being made prior to the evocation of privacy as our best defense, and these prior assumptions are analogous to those made by data-centric corporations, institutions, and practitioners regarding the data itself.

---

10. Deleuze 1992.
11. Heidegger 1977.
12. See, for example: Caputo 1987; Heidegger 1996; Gadamer 1997.
13. Cheney-Lippold 2017.

I suggest there are at least three assumptions that ground the so-called right to privacy that can be understood as analogous to those of the data-centric industry. These are: 1) Data are information-facts; 2) Data is something one already holds in possession prior to its extraction; 3) If we and the data we possess can be protected from extraction, then we can maintain possession of it for our own use, enjoyment, or profit. That is, we can benefit from its useful-value. I will consider each of these in turn.

Assumption 1: *Data are information-facts.* Just as the data-centric industry considers data as observable, extractable, categorizable, and indexable information-facts in the world, so too the right to privacy assumes that data are already existing information-facts in the world. Both the data-centric industry and right to privacy advocates seem to share a basic definition of a fact, which is the quality of being actual, that is, already there in existence whether as real or imagined. Just as a chair, a coffee mug, or my daydream of lying under a palm tree on a quiet beach are facts in this sense, so too data are considered as just this. Indeed, from the perspective of both the data-centric industries and right to privacy advocates, these facts and data are essentially equated. By means of a well-designed analysis of this text (according to the data science textbook quoted above), it could be concluded that there is at least one chair and a filled coffee mug in the space within which the author currently is, and the author is a person who daydreams about beaches. These are "useful insights," or facts and data, about the author and the space he currently occupies that could be extracted and sold for profit.

Furthermore, there is an assumed transparency, literalness, and transitive fidelity to these data as information-facts. That is to say, the fact is clear and distinct in its existence; its meaning is similarly clear and distinct, and thus without ambiguity or interpretation. Therefore, the transparency and literalness of the fact will transition without remainder or excess, that is, with fidelity, into data. The result: data=information-facts. Again, this is an assumption held by both advocates of the right to privacy and the data-centric industry.

Assumption 2: *Data is something one already holds in possession prior to its extraction.* Just as we could say (at least metaphorically) that prior to the mining process the coalfield "possesses" the coal, so too advocates of the right to privacy assume that we possess our information-facts prior to their extraction by the data-centric industry. For many of these advocates, possession is articulated in terms of ownership and, as we will see below, in terms of monetary value. Thus, for example, one of the better-known positions of data privacy—Alex Pentland's "New Deal on Data"—is articulated in terms of defining *who owns data*.[14] While Pentland's argument may be one of the more obvious articulations of this assumption, ownership as private property possession is the grounding assumption of all right to privacy arguments.

Thus, for example, the assumption is made that my daydream as an information-fact is mine and only mine, and as such I have a right to it. What is this right? At the very least it entails the right to daydream at all. As a kind of being with the capacity to daydream, it is my right to do so. But since anyone could have a daydream, this right must be more specific. As such, my right is to this *particular* daydream, and, most importantly, what it indicates about my fantasies, my emotions and moods, goals and hopes. That is to say, about me as a singular person.

In other words, my right to privacy regarding this particular daydream is founded upon a Lockean conception of my right to the property of my own person, property here meaning not just possession but dominion.[15] This particular daydream as indicative of my singular personhood is a fact that I possess/own because I possess my very person, and as such, I have a right to it. But it is precisely the assumption of the fact of the daydream as indicative of my personhood that makes it particularly appealing for extraction by the data-centric industry. Thus, the very basis for making a rights claim on the daydream is precisely the same basis for its extractive value.

Assumption 3: *If we and the information-facts we possess can be protected from extraction, then we can maintain possession of them for our own use, enjoyment, or profit, that is, for their useful-value.* As that which I possess and have dominion over, I—and only I—can use my daydream as I see fit. For example, I can keep the daydream to myself and enjoy the temporary respite from writing this essay; or I can share this daydream with my spouse and we can fantasize together about fulfilling it someday; or I can use it as inspiration for a bad painting that I would make on the weekend; or I could use it as motivation to leave behind academia and open a bar on a beach such that selling drinks under palm trees will help fulfill the hope that I could spend my life under one; or I could simply

---

14.   Pentland 2009; see also Zuboff 2019: 441.
15.   Locke 1980; see also Zigon 2018: chapter 1.

sell to some data-centric company or practitioner the fact that I had this daydream, along with any number of other facts about myself.

The point being that as my possession, I have the right to do what I please with the fact of my daydream. Similarly, once extracted, the data-centric industry treats my daydream as an information-fact that it puts to use in any way it finds valuable. In both cases, the daydream's existence is rendered little more than useful-value placed in standing-reserve.

If these three assumptions are accurate, then the right to privacy response to the extraction imperative of the data-centric industries is ultimately the wrong response to the problem I outlined above. For ethics properly conceived cannot result in the perpetuation of the status quo, even if with a slightly better situation (however better is defined in each problematic situation). Rather, ethics—as an ongoing process of living together well—must result in a shift of the very world that we inhabit together. In the rest of this chapter, I will begin to outline what I conceive as a properly ethical response to the problem of data surveillance and extraction.

Data as Given

What is data? In Latin, *data* is the plural form of *datum*, which means "something given," as well as "a present or gift." How does thinking of data in these terms shift the way in which we consider ethics in relation to data? To begin with, we immediately discern a modification to the relationality of a data-centric situation. Whereas the paradigm outlined above begins from the extraction and capture of data as information-facts already there *in toto* in the world, my proposed modification entails data as that which is given—and given not as fact but as gift. Whereas the paradigm of data as information-facts to be extracted and captured leads to an "ethical" concern focused on protection and defense of this data as if it were property over which one had dominion, data as the given invokes an ethical demand on the receiver to respond. As such, we witness a shift from an ethics of (property) defense to a relational ethics of the gift.

Who is the receiver in this new paradigm of data as the given? Indeed, who is the giver? The first and easy reply would be that the giver is me, you, and everyone else from whom data is extracted, and thus, the receiver would be all those data extractors. But this conflates the data as information-fact paradigm with the one we are thinking through here.

For we remain within the binary distinction between the one that gives that which is possessed and the one that receives and becomes the new possessor. This conflation returns us—perhaps a bit more sophisticatedly—to where we began, that is, stuck in an "ethics" of (property) defense.

To liberate our thought from this paradigm, it will be helpful to consider a bit more closely that which is given. For only in doing so can we leave behind both the very idea of data as information-fact, as well as the "ethics" that leaves us stuck in this binary thinking of the situation. Phenomenology—and particularly the work of Jean-Luc Marion—will be particularly insightful for thinking data as the given, and ultimately, for a relational ethics of the gift.

Building on the work of classical phenomenology that emphasized the givenness of phenomena, Marion argues that "what *shows itself* first *gives itself*."[16] In particular, Marion draws heavily from Husserl's work on the phenomenological reduction and modes of givenness, as well as Heidegger's definition of a phenomenon as that which "shows itself in itself," or, as he also put it, as that which gives itself (*Es gibt*).[17] That is, in contrast to a metaphysics of objectivity that assumes that phenomena are always already there *in toto* in the world to be discovered and used for some purpose—a metaphysics that grounds data-centric practices— phenomenology begins with phenomena that give themselves and do so always only in part or as hermeneutical aspects of themselves. This is true whether the phenomenon is a rock, a coffee mug, climate, traffic patterns, a disease, an emotion, a thought, a Facebook "like," one's marriage status, or, indeed, even one's "self." What data-centric practitioners call data, then, is what phenomenologists call phenomena, with the important caveat that the former cover over the aspectual and hermeneutic phenomenality of phenomena by considering them as totalized and objectified information-facts.

All phenomena, by definition, show themselves by giving themselves temporarily and partially. Every giving of a phenomenon is simultaneously a withdrawal of that very same phenomenon. The phenomenon, therefore, can never be known, understood, extracted, analyzed, coded, or used in total. In other words, all phenomena exist in excess of what we can experience of them. Consequently, anything that we can claim "to know" about a phenomenon is a matter of a situated interpretation of that which gives itself in part. What is now commonly referred to as

---

16.   Marion 2002: 5; italics in original.
17.   Husserl 1962; Heidegger 1996: 25.

bias in data-centric practices and technologies is the result of ignoring the situated interpretive relationship we necessarily always have with all phenomena.

Importantly, for Marion phenomena give themselves without condition.[18] That which gives itself as itself does so without the limitation or imposition of a prior rule, principle, horizon, or subject.[19] It is only through a situated interpretive relationship that a phenomenon is brought under the order of meaning. Meaning never arises along with that which gives itself, but only comes to be by means of how that which is already given is acknowledged and recognized. Therefore, it is easy to understand that in a contemporary condition characterized by metaphysical humanism, all phenomena have come to be understood as objective information-facts waiting to be utilized for some purpose. Indeed, this contemporary condition says nothing about the phenomena themselves other than that they objectively preexist as standing-reserve for our use. In contrast, phenomenology begins with the assumption that nothing can be said of phenomenality as such other than that it gives itself. What can eventually be said, however, concerns the situated interpretations through which phenomena manifest meaningfully. But when these interpretations are rendered as objective information-facts (data) by data-practitioners, then this is akin to these very practitioners holding a mirror up to themselves and naming the reflected image truth.[20]

Does it make sense, then, to ask who are the giver and receiver if we understand phenomenality in this way? No. For there is no "who" of givenness. The givenness of phenomenality precedes all subjectivity and interpretation, and that which gives itself does so to a receiver (or what Marion calls the gifted). Consequently, we can say that the "data" that might otherwise be considered "mine"—for example, my gender or my mood—is given to "me"; it precedes that which can legitimately be called my "self" at any given moment. As a first response to the question of giver and receiver, then, it could be said that "I" am both receiver and giver in that "I" both receive, for example, my gender and give it. Such a response, however, entails a logic of possessive causality and a difficult-to-shake assumption of agentive capacity, such that "I" come to possess that which "I" receive, and then have the "right" to give it as "I" please.

---

18. Marion 2002: 320.
19. Marion 2002: 17–18.
20. Cf. Rorty 1979.

Here we are back again at an "ethics" of (property) defense, even if the binarism of a simple receiver-giver relation is broken.

When we take seriously phenomenality as that which gives itself partially and temporarily prior to any subjectivity, however, "I" can only ever be a receiver of that which is given and can never give it in turn. As such, ontologically I must be open to the phenomenality of givenness; ethically I must attune to it; and politically I must respond with justice. This onto-ethical-political relationality maintains the openness of givenness in a mutuality of existence. "I" remain forever a receiver of the unfolding of givenness that affects "me," and it is precisely this reception that becomes "me" in every moment. "My" ongoing onto-ethical-political response to these affects is indicative of this status as receiver.

When such responsivity, attunement, and justice break down, however, the "I" emerges as object. This is precisely what data-centric practices do—they break down responsivity, attunement, and justice, thus rendering the objectification of the human self. Or to use the language of data-practitioners, the relationality of human experience is objectified as manipulatable behavior. Thus, the open receptivity that is human experience is shut down, closed off, and mined as a source for extractive accumulation.

This is not a matter of data-centric practitioners becoming the receivers and we the givers. Rather, this is a matter of the former being exploitative takers and the rest of us rendered raw material in the process. The givenness of phenomenality is shut down. The relationality of givenness is cut. The attuned-justice of relational ethical-politics is disfigured into an "ethics" of (property) defense, perhaps better understood as economics.

From Economics to Relational Ethics and Justice

Today, such a pretense of ethics is regularly offered as our best defense against surveillance capitalism. Perhaps the most telling example is a fairly recent piece of legislation presented in the United States Senate in response to the extraction-for-profit *modus operandi* of the data-centric industry. The DASHBOARD Act introduced in June 2019 by Senators Mark R. Warner and Josh Hawley "will require data harvesting companies such as social media platforms to tell consumers and financial regulators exactly what data they are collecting from consumers, and how it is being leveraged by the platform for profit."[21] The central focus of the DASHBOARD Act is the monetary value of data collected. Thus, as it is summarized on Senator Warner's website, the Act will require "commercial data operators (defined as services with over 100 million monthly active users) to disclose types of data collected as well as regularly provide their users with an *assessment of the value* of that data." Furthermore, it will require "commercial data operators to file an annual report on the *aggregate value* of user data they've collected, as well as contracts with third parties involving data collection."[22]

Although the transparency required by the DASHBOARD Act is laudable, its focus on the value and monetary aspect of data is problematic. As the anthropologist Samuel Lengen has argued in his commentary on the DASHBOARD Act, "estimating the value of user data isn't simple" and neither will it solve privacy issues.[23] This is so because, as Lengen rightly puts it, data is extremely difficult to valuate, and privacy is no longer a matter of personal data because any particular personal data now implicates any number of others' data. There are two important points here: 1) data has no inherent worth of its own—and indeed, despite its monetization may be an-economic; and 2) data is relational—that is, all data is intertwined with other persons and things such that there is no personal data as such.

And yet, such an Act (or one like it) is precisely the kind of response many call for in their concern for data ethics and policy. Unfortunately, the DASHBOARD Act is an economic response masquerading as an ethical one. The assumption of the Act is that if the value of one's data is transparent, and one can opt out of having one's data monetized, then this constitutes data ethics. But note, this is just another iteration of the ethics-as-property defense that I outlined above. Much as a homeowner receives a property valuation estimate each year from their city, so too under the Act each person will receive a valuation of their personal data and have the choice to "defend" that property by "protecting" it from

---

21. "Warner & Hawley Introduce Bill to Force Social Media Companies to Disclose How They Are Monetizing User Data." Senator Mark R. Warner webpage, press releases, June 24, 2019. https://www.warner.senate.gov/public/index.cfm/2019/6/warner-hawley-introduce-bill-to-force-social-media-companies-to-disclose-how-they-are-monetizing-user-data (last accessed July 19, 2023).

22. Ibid.; italics added.

23. Lengen 2019.

others using it for their economic gain. To the extent that this could be called an ethics at all (and I certainly would not call it that) it is an "ethics" of the fence or wall as it does little more than create the illusion that it is possible to isolate oneself by cutting off relationality.

But we have come to see that data are the multifarious relational manifestations of the givenness of phenomenality. Thus, when we think data as the given—that is, when we preserve the phenomenality of the given—what is the proper ethics that accompanies this thinking? Recall that data as the given is *not* an object already standing there in the world waiting to be "given" to (that is, taken by) the first human to come along with the means to grasp it. Rather, data as the given gives itself as itself as a gift. Consequently, there is a certain kind of privilege bestowed upon the receiver, or in Marion's terms, the gifted. To receive the gift of phenomenality—whether it manifests as the daydream of laying on the beach, the desire and act of "liking" a Facebook post, or even as pain in the lower back—to receive any gift of phenomenality indicates the privilege of being the kind of being that exists as an open receiver of the world. Such a privilege entails an ethical demand. And yet, we must be careful not to respond to this demand with an "ethics" that is little more than economics well disguised.

Marcel Mauss famously articulated the gift in terms of the demand of a return. That is, the gift entails an obligation to reciprocate. Indeed, in an earlier work on gifts, Mauss described his forthcoming essay, *The Gift*, as "a work on 'the obligation to return presents,'"[24] and in the opening pages of his famous essay he writes that the problem with which he will deal is that of what "compels the gift that has been received to be obligatorily reciprocated?"[25] Furthermore, Mauss described this demand of reciprocity in the following manner: "This system presupposes (1) the obligation to give; (2) the obligation to receive; (3) the obligation to repay."[26]

Although *The Gift* concludes with some remarks on morality, the essay's overwhelming emphasis and discussion of modes of economic exchange make it rather clear that Mauss is not so much describing the ethics of the gift as givenness, as he is a total "system" (institution) of economic exchange in terms of obligation.[27] In other words, for

---

24. Mauss 1997: 31.
25. Mauss 1990: 3.
26. Quoted in Marion 2002: 343; see also Mauss 1990.
27. Marion 2002: 75–79; see also Derrida 1992b.

Mauss the gift loses its very status as an indication of the phenom- enality of givenness, and becomes, in turn, a material causal marker of systemic obligations. Thus, rather than an ethics emerging from the very givenness of the gift, Mauss is articulating a system of economic exchange founded on the causal logic of sufficient reason.[28] Mauss, then, is not describing an ethics but an economics masquerading as ethics.

A relational ethics adequate to givenness, in contrast, would main- tain and attune to ever-unfolding relations without the obligation of a reciprocal return—without debt. For Marion—as it was for Derrida— it could not be otherwise if we are to take seriously the noneconomic nature of ethics. And yet, a relational ethics *does* entail a transitive response such that that which is received is not possessed but passed on. Lisa Guenther has articulated such an ethics as follows: "this gift does not belong to me but rather commands me to give to Others."[29] And yet, if that which is given—the datum—cannot be reciprocally returned for risk of reducing ethics to an economics, then to whom or what could the given gift be passed? In other words, to whom or what could the receiver become the giver such that the new receiver does not—indeed, cannot—reciprocate but becomes yet another giver to whom or whatever arrives next? For Marion, one possible response is the community.

To give to the community is to give to an existent that cannot recip- rocate the gift, thus maintaining the ethical nature of relationality. This is so because the community as receiver is absent and is so for at least two reasons.[30] First, when the community is receiver, "no individual can be set up as universal" receiver such that she could stand in for the com- munity to accept on behalf of it or to say thank you. Second, the com- munity as receiver is absent because it can only accept the gift for the sake of transmitting it "toward givees still to come."[31] The community as receiver, then, can never be made manifest in the person of any one individual or group of individuals, for a community is an open being- with-in-common that transmits the gift to those who will one day arrive. In this way, Marion tells us, the gift "achieves its perfect figure: it is given without distinguishing among persons, in complete indifference to the

---

28. Marion 2002: 75.
29. Guenther 2006: 3.
30. Marion 2002: 93.
31. Marion 2002: 93.

worthiness or unworthiness of the receiver, in complete ignorance of any possible reciprocity."[32]

Such a relational ethics of the gift resonates well with recent attempts within continental philosophy to rethink the notion of community in terms of openness and givenness.[33] This notion of community contrasts with the more typical conception of community as localized, totalized, and closed that was common throughout most of twentieth-century social and political theory, and which can be understood as a response to the alienating and exclusionary fragmentation of modernity.[34] Although anthropologists have more recently tended to be critical of this traditional conception of community,[35] Rupert Stasch convincingly shows that traces of it linger in many of the discipline's most dearly held concepts and analytic approaches.[36]

Roberto Esposito, in contrast to this traditional conception, has offered the most noteworthy contribution to the new literature on community.[37] For Esposito, community is characterized by a mutual obligation to care outside any notion of debt or expectation. Contrasting his conception of community with what he calls the immunitary logic of biopolitics—the logic of inclusive exclusion—Esposito articulates an affirmative biopolitics grounded on the open vulnerability of finite existence and the community such existence demands. Esposito describes this notion of community by considering the etymological constitution of *communitas* in terms of the *cum* of being-with and the *munus* of the obligatory care that such being-with entails. This obligation to care, Esposito emphasizes, takes the form of the nonreciprocal gift. Community, then, is the being-with-in-common that obliges care in the form of a gift; a gift, that is, in the form of nonreciprocal giving to whoever arrives. Relational ethics as I am articulating it in this chapter and book, then, is the kind of ethics that makes such a community possible.

There are, perhaps, similarities here to some anthropological conceptions of reciprocity, for example, the generalized reciprocity of Marshall

---

32. Marion 2002: 94.
33. See, for example: Blanchot 1988; Nancy 1991; Agamben 2009; Esposito 2010; Zigon 2019.
34. Wolin 2004: 325; see also Anderson 1999; Bauman 2001.
35. See, for example: Gupta and Ferguson 1992.
36. Stasch 2009.
37. Esposito 2013.

Sahlins[38] or the redistributive reciprocity most famously exemplified by the potlatch. Still, in addition to the clear economic focus of these conceptions of reciprocity, they differ from the ethical relationality I am trying to describe in that both forms of reciprocity involve specific givers and receivers, even if they are temporally, spatially, and/or hierarchically differentiated. More interestingly, there are some similarities between the relational ethics of the gift that I am articulating here and what anthropologist Merav Shohet calls asymmetrical reciprocity. She describes such reciprocity as the way in which "multiple generations come to view one another as bound in relations of [moral] debt, including to one's deceased ancestors and not yet born descendants." But even in this description—and similar ones Shohet offers—reciprocity is described in terms of "relations of moral *debt* and *obligation*."[39] This coupling of debt and obligation, I suggest, makes it very difficult to deny the trace of economics in this conception of reciprocity, despite the author's assertions otherwise.

In contrast, I am trying to articulate the transitivity of ethical relationality as a giving that creates an openness for what or whoever comes next outside of any sense of debt. This transitivity, then, may be better described in terms of hospitality. The anthropologist Saiba Varma, for example, contrasts Mauss's conception of the gift, which is "laden with expectations of return," with hospitality, which is "nonreciprocal" and "in its ideal form, should be given without expectation."[40] What I want to emphasize, then, is that as the never fully present receiver of the gift, the community only ever receives the gift to transmit it to its not-yet and differentiable future manifestation unburdened by debt. This is what Marion describes as "a forever future givee."[41] We could also describe it as a form of radical hospitality.

What might this look like in our data-centric world? Let us consider a brief imagined scenario based on the back pain example I offered earlier. As one typically does these days, you might search on Google for various ways to address your back pain. Almost immediately you start seeing ads appear in your social media or online newspaper or email platform for such things as new mattresses, new couches, supportive shoes, foam

---

38. Sahlins 1972.
39. Shohet 2021: 72–73; my italics.
40. Varma 2020: 181. See also: Derrida 1999; Derrida and Dufourmantelle 2000.
41. Marion 2002: 93.

rollers, and yoga pants. This is a common occurrence within surveillance capitalism that likely every reader has experienced. In the scenario I'm envisioning, your data would still be collected—I think we are past the threshold of stopping that, and perhaps we don't really want to—but rather than being fed back to us as advertisements, it would be passed on to "future givees" as possible evidence that Americans seem to have a lot of back problems.

While this relational ethics of the gift would not project onto these "future givees" an expectation of what they ought to do with this data, one possible scenario could be the following: rather than addressing this back problem epidemic through consumption, perhaps instead it could be addressed by changing policies and social practices that likely result in excessive back pain. For example, food production that too easily leads to obesity, labor regimes and lifestyles that entail too much sitting, infrastructure that emphasizes driving over walking or biking. Or "future givees" may interpret the data in a completely other manner—perhaps they may interpret it to mean that Americans have too much time on their hands and therefore do too many internet searches. Consequently, they may find other ways to fill all this extra time being wasted on internet searches. Or perhaps they may simply ignore the data.

This scenario that results in various possibilities rather than a definitive obligation may be disappointing for some readers. But this is precisely the point of an ethics of the gift as a form of radical hospitality—the gift/data is given without expectation, without debt. Instead, this relational ethics and hospitality offers an opportunity to exercise what Varma calls "moral imagination."[42] Above all, it offers the possibility of hope. For to give otherwise is no longer ethics, but rather a species of economic accounting.

Some Closing Words

This chapter has attempted to articulate a relational ethics and justice adequate to our data-centric worlds. In doing so, it was necessary to break out of the economics (and thus, debt) of reciprocity so as to transcend the binarism of giver and receiver in the recognition that a relational ethics and justice demands that those or that which receive in the future remain unknown. Furthermore, it is imperative to note that precisely

---

42. Varma 2020: 194.

what the community-to-come receives also remains unknown. For to maintain the ethicality of the gift and not slip back into the transaction of economics, that which is received by the future receiver must remain unknown. For neither ethics nor justice are a matter of following a rule, principle, or criterion, but rather a matter of attuning to situations and others as they arrive. How we respond can never be known prior to the demand of the moment. This is the risk of ethics. Similarly, although we may know that our data as gift will be received in some form or another by those yet to arrive, we hold no rights over how our data/gift will appear or how it will be received. Only as such can the relational ethics of the gift refuse the form of a transaction and instead be an offer of justice.

We have crossed the threshold of a data-centric and data-driven society, a threshold across which there is no return. Consequently, it is imperative to recognize that the only ethics adequate to a data society begins not with the individualism of privacy (that mirrors the individualism of profit), but rather with the relationality of the datum as gift. This chapter has shown that the only ethics and justice adequate to a data-centric society are relational in their ongoing attunement to that which is given as it is passed on to the community-to-come and to those yet to arrive. Put another way, the data-centric society demands radical hospitality.

CHAPTER 5

Ethics Beyond the Human

"It is legitimate to say that I'm worried about climate change, and that's a mood," Dipesh Chakrabarty recently told an interviewer.[1] Increasingly, few would disagree, though they might perhaps question the cause of the change. Still, it is difficult to deny this mood and the sense of looming disaster it portends.[2] We should listen to our moods. For, as Jason Throop puts it, moods are "always attuned to the at times difficult to trace conditions—personal, interpersonal, situational, and historical—within which individuals and communities find themselves."[3] Put another way, moods are indicative of how it is between us. For good reason, then, we must learn to be attentive to moods. For they are perhaps the clearest indication of how well one is attuned and attuned to in turn.

According to Throop, moods can be indicative of a moral breakdown.[4] Similarly, Chakrabarty describes the mood climate change has induced for him—perhaps for many of us—as the "shock of the Anthropocene," which signals what he calls a "breach" in "the usual assumption of a relationship of mutuality between humans and the 'earth.'"[5] This breach—this moral breakdown—that is increasingly felt by more and

---

1.   Chakrabarty 2015.
2.   Throop 2022.
3.   Throop 2020: 68.
4.   Throop 2014.
5.   Chakrabarty 2021: 192, 182.

more of us demands a response. And yet, too often our response is a nonresponse.

Perhaps this is because when we heed our mood today, many of us cannot help but recognize it as despair. This recognition is important. For Throop explains that despair is "an attunement to a condition of *radical vulnerability* whereby we find ourselves exposed to, and wounded by" the loss of possibilities.[6] This loss is not simply that of the looming loss of the climate disaster, but the loss of a world of possibilities. To be more precise for the purposes of this book: the despair many feel today is brought on by the fact that our traditional ethical resources are inadequate not just to the contemporary condition of our worlds but most especially to our planetary existence. If our response to today's political possibilities is one of disappointment—as I put in a recent book of that title[7]—then our response to our available ethical (non)possibilities is that of despair.

Faced by this despair brought about by the recognition that as human we are always already radically vulnerable and exposed, I will argue that we must begin to think an ethics that both includes and extends beyond the human.[8] This is an ethics that in attuning to the situational between of assembled existents—human and nonhuman alike—attends to and leaves open possibilities for the continued unfolding of each of us. Consequently, this is a relational ethics that is indicative of an existential imperative to dwell on this planet with others—*all* others. Put another way, the last, best hope against despair—and, perhaps, against the various looming planetary catastrophes we are exposed to—is a relational ethics.

This book began as a response to Jean-Luc Nancy's call for an ethics of the world. I have been referring to such an ethics as relational because worlds emerge as one expression of a relational ontology of what Nancy calls being-with: "existence *is with*: otherwise nothing exists."[9] I have been trying to articulate an ethics adequate to this withness of existence. I have been trying to articulate an ethics of the world that might follow from Nancy's claim that "a world is this: that everything is here and demands to be greeted insofar as it's here [and that] evil is precisely

---

6.   Throop 2020: 65; italics in original.

7.   Zigon 2018.

8.   For a provocation on the imperative of moods for environmental ethics, see Trigg 2014.

9.   Nancy 2000: 4.

refusing the world, wanting to substitute an empire for it."[10] This entails a more capacious conception of both *ethics* and *world*. For this would be an ethics of the world that welcomes hospitably those existents that have been traditionally (at least in the so-called Western tradition) excluded from both ethics and world. Put another way: this is an ethics of open hospitality that welcomes all existents into our worlds *without* reducing them to a human conception; an ethics that lets-be and attunes rather than projects and controls. How do we respond to the demand made by all existents to be greeted as here—as one of us—in a world?

My claim has been that our traditional human-centric conceptions of ethics—and politics—fail to meet this demand, and, in fact, have to a great extent resulted in the substitution of the world for empire; that is, a conceptually human-centric empire that understands everything as merely there as standing-reserve to be put to calculative use for the pleasure of (a certain small sliver of) humanity. In contrast, throughout this book I have been trying to think and articulate a relational ethics that begins not with the human but with the between that connects us all—human and nonhuman alike. Thus, in contrast to asking traditional ethical questions—such as, what is the good? or did she act rightly?—I have argued that the most fundamental of all ethical (and thus, political) questions is: how is it between us?

In doing so, I ended each of the first three chapters of this book with a provocation that gave way to the final two chapters, in which I have been thinking the possibility of a relational ethics and justice beyond the human. The second chapter concluded with the thought that perhaps we are better off moving beyond a conception of truth. For today, our worlds more than ever call us to think, and in so doing place a demand upon us to become ethical beings striving for a sense of worlds that are increasingly complex. This complexity arises not simply from the in-creased technological dominance of our worlds, but from the increased realization of the relational interdependence of existence as such. The possibility of truth slips beyond our grasp within such complexity; thus, we must hone our capacity to sense and think the world.

Nancy articulates this relationality of existence by means of sense when he writes that what "existence strives toward is the world and Be-ing-in-the-world, that is, toward the possibility of making sense. Sense is the reference of all existences between each other . . . one must know how

---

10.   Nancy 2017: 134.

to think sense in all its forms, living and non-living."[11] Foreshadowing this thought, Maurice Merleau-Ponty in his late work on relational ontology wrote that the between is that chiasmatic intertwining where the other-in-self crosses over and connects with the self-in-other (what or whoever self and other may be).[12] If sense is this chiasmic intertwining of existents between one another—and if we have any hope for a future other than apocalypse—then we must ask and adequately answer the following: how must we attune such that we humans do our part for allowing all existents to dwell trustingly in worlds of "common" sense? This question pushes beyond ethics, or perhaps better put, it reveals that as an ethical being one is also a political being in that "the political is the place of the in-common as such . . . the place of being-*together*"[13] for all existents.

This is, of course, the demand of justice. In considering justice relationally, the third chapter ended with the thought that the demand of justice is best considered in terms of attunement. Our response to this demand—our acting justly—must be, I argued, our attuning to—without eradicating—the constellation of differences that is social existence. And as I tried to show in both that third and the fourth chapter, any justice that does not ultimately descend into an algorithm can be nothing other than the constant struggle to keep attuning. For there may be temporary moments of lingering together in the attuned justice of consideration and care, but one thing history tells us is certain, a new demand for justice will soon arrive. When it does, we must, once again, respond.

A new and alien demand has arrived. Paradoxically, this is also the oldest, closest, and most unavoidably persistent demand. And yet, it has been systematically covered over, ignored, and forgotten for a very long time. Existence has always demanded justice, but does so differently and by new names each time it calls out to us. Today this existential demand for justice goes by the name of the planet. Chakrabarty has argued compellingly that the humanities and social sciences must begin taking the planet seriously as a focus of thought. Since, according to Chakrabarty, the planet decenters the human, it differs from the globe, which he describes as a "humanocentric construction." And yet, the planet as "a dynamic ensemble of relationships" remains "the condition of human

---

11.   Nancy 2017: 133–34.
12.   Merleau-Ponty 1997; see also Toadvine 2009.
13.   Nancy 1997: 88; italics in original.

existence."[14] This is the planet that calls for justice. This is the planet that demands an ethical response as part of our world. Indeed, if we are going to take seriously the conceptions of moral assemblage and radical hospitality that I articulated in the third and fourth chapters, then we must begin to hear and respond to the planet as an ethical being striving along with us for a world and demanding to be greeted as such, as Jean-Luc Nancy might put it.

Many hear the planet's call but respond in all-too-human ways. Some respond—out of habit, perhaps—with economy and technology (tax credits and carbon capture, for example); others respond in the most moral way they know how (deontological duties toward the environment or granting rights to rivers and forests, for example). But each of these are responses that continue the tendency to "anthropomorphize nature," as Nietzsche observed already quite some time ago.[15] They are continuations of a worldview that conceives nonhuman (and, indeed, human) existence as standing-reserve there for calculative use (even if in its preservation).

If we hope one day to respond to the question of "how is it between us?" in terms that are not indicative of empire (that is, war and control), then we must begin to imagine, think, and enact an ethics and politics beyond the human. An ethics and politics, that is, that are not just another projection of alleged human attributes onto nonhumans (e.g., principles, rights, parliaments), but rather ones that express the relational between that constitutes the worlds we all share, human and nonhuman alike. I concluded the first chapter of this book by noting that if in 1958 Hannah Arendt could limit the between to the human condition, then in the twenty-first century that is no longer possible. For today it has become clear that the between is essential to the existential condition. The between can no longer be limited to between you and me. Rather, we must come to recognize the between of existence as such. And yet, despite all our posthuman desires and fantasies, how humans respond to the call of this existential between will be decisive.

And this is precisely the point. The posthuman fantasies that have driven much contemporary theory seem to forget that it is the being we call human that causes much of the damage and crisis with which we are concerned. The damage and crisis will not disappear through the projection of all-too-human capacities onto nonhuman existents—for

---

14. Chakrabarty 2021: 4, 70.
15. Babich 2015: 87.

example, the thinking of forests or the responsibility of photons.[16] Rather, the damage and crisis of our contemporary catastrophic times can only be addressed by recognizing the failure of humans to respond to the demand for justice made by the planet. Perhaps the new ethics and politics we need today—a relational ethics and politics—is simply another way of acknowledging the human failure to respond appropriately to this demand. So then, how do we respond to this demand for justice? Do we continue to project our already established criteria—rights, duties, responsibility—onto the between? Or do we let-be and attune? If "how is it between us?" is the most fundamental question, then how we respond to it must be the most fundamental of ethical—as well as political—as well as existential—replies.

Attunement Beyond the Human

It has become commonplace to respond to this demand of the planet—this demand of existence—in an all-too-human manner. This is, of course, to be expected from more traditional ethical theorists who variously articulate, for example, deontological or utilitarian responses to the climate and environmental disasters of our day.[17] Strangely, however, so-called posthumanist theorists also tend to respond in the same manner, without, of course acknowledging, or perhaps even recognizing themselves, that they do so.[18] Many posthumanists would likely agree with Marjolein Oele's call for an ethics that focuses "our attention on the emergent co-relationships between beings," and a politics by which "the various forms of affective lives and their interdependence are given a chance for transformation."[19] Too often, however, posthumanists attempt to do so using human-centric concepts such as responsibility and care, or in the explicit conclusion made by Jane Bennett to proceed

---

16. See Kohn 2013; Barad 2007.
17. For excellent critical overview of this literature and phenomenological, hermeneutic, deconstructive, and pragmatist alternatives, see: Brown and Toadvine 2003; Toadvine 2009; Clingerman et al. 2014; Fritsch, Lynes, and Wood 2018; Sorgen 2021.
18. See, for example, my critique of Barad (2007) and Bennett (2010) in Zigon 2018: chapter 5.
19. Oele 2020: 6.

with "a careful course of anthropomorphization."[20] I am extremely sympathetic to the difficulty of thinking and writing ethical and political theory beyond the human. I also recognize that ultimately it may not even by possible. For I also recognize—as I have argued extensively in *Disappointment*—that all concepts come with a proclivity to repeat their foundational meaning despite attempts to "rethink" them.[21] Because of this conceptual proclivity, I have argued that we are better off eschewing the attempt to "rethink," and instead should take up the difficult task of concept creation. Put another way, posthumanism will only be a successful theoretical strategy when it leaves behind human-centric concepts and creates new ones adequate to a nonhuman-centric existence.

For example, in his important book, *How Forests Think*, Eduardo Kohn compellingly shows how we can begin to conceive an "us" beyond the human. Kohn argues that a central aspect of what he calls an anthropology beyond the human is "to recognize those opportunities where an *us* that exceeds the limits of individual bodies, species, and even concrete existence can come to extend beyond the present. This *us*—and the hopeful worlds it beckons us to imagine and realize—is an open whole."[22] By including all of life in the *us* that is a relational web of habituated relationality, Kohn's singular work is helpful for conceiving that when we ask how it is between us, we include within that question those and that which extend beyond the human.

Kohn creatively reads Charles Sanders Peirce along with his own long-term ethnographic research with the Runa of Ecuador's Upper Amazon to articulate a semiotic theory of life. In particular, he takes up what the linguistic anthropologist Alejandro Paz calls the "weird" Peirce, which are those parts of the latter's oeuvre "that reach beyond the human to situate representation in the workings and logics of a broader nonhuman universe out of which we humans come."[23] Such a reading allows Kohn to claim that forests think—indeed, all of life thinks—because representational processes are the "basis for all thought" and all "life-forms represent the world in some way or another, and these

---

20. Bennett 2010: 122.
21. Zigon 2018.
22. Kohn 2013; italics in original.
23. Kohn 2013: 7–8.

representations are intrinsic to their being."[24] For this reason, Kohn concludes not only that "life is inherently semiotic," but that as such life *is* thought.[25]

Kohn convincingly reads his ethnographic research through this semiotic theory to show that forest life—nonhuman animals, trees, plants, and humans among them—is inextricably connected through what he calls a web of habits. Such habits can be considered as something like an accumulation of embodied semiotic interpretations over time. Indeed, for Kohn life "proliferates habits" as particular life-forms "represent and amplify" already existing habits of the world and create new ones through their multifarious "interactions with other organisms." Becoming relationally attuned to such habits and their unfolding over time is central to Kohn's conception of how one becomes "aligned with a broader 'us.'"[26]

Much of this is compelling and broadly resonates with the aim and arguments of this book, and particularly this chapter. Still, I am concerned by Kohn's insistence that we conceive of this relational and interpretive ontology in terms of thinking. Certainly, Kohn over and over assures the reader that he does not intend thinking in human terms. Yet, one must wonder if Kohn doth protest too much. For despite the constant assurances and his fascinating argumentation, the burden is ultimately put on the reader to accept as a premise that thinking is not a human privilege. Indeed, even if the reader does accept this premise, the conceptual proclivity of "thinking" entails that it is nearly impossible not to notice the irrepressible traces of its human-centricity.

For it turns out that not only forests think but they are populated with all kinds of anthropomorphisms—logic, mind, representations, meaning, and nonhuman persons and selves, among others. As these continue to pile up throughout the book, it becomes increasingly difficult not to allow suspicions of anthropomorphism to creep in—even if it is done a bit more carefully, as Bennett suggests. For example, speaking of nonhuman life, Kohn tells us that for Peirce "the Cartesian *cogito*, the 'I think,' is not exclusively human, nor is it housed inside the mind."[27] He also tells us that "selves [including nonhuman ones], in short, are thoughts."[28] How are these claims any different than the Cartesian "I think, therefore I

---

24. Kohn 2013: 7, 9.
25. Kohn 2013: 74 (Kohn makes this point throughout the book).
26. Kohn 2013: 62.
27. Kohn 2013: 87.
28. Kohn 2013: 83.

am," other than the extension of thought and selfhood into the nonhuman realm? How is the reader who is not already a posthumanist true believer to think that this is anything other than a metaphysical humanist projection onto the nonhuman?

We must be aware of the conceptual proclivity of the concepts we take up. For the articulation and enactment of concepts tend to lead to certain kinds of results despite the intentions of those who adopt them. And this is so because concepts over time come to contain within them, as it were, a proclivity that repeatedly becomes instrumentalized in similar ways. That is, they contain a proclivity that results in the concept being mobilized for similar ends within similar subjective and power constellations, and thus repeat and perpetuate the ontological tradition that is the ground of such constellations. Therefore, it is not good enough to "rethink" our concepts as Kohn and others commonly argue we must; try as we like, we will not be able to shake the conceptual proclivity of the concept. Rather, we must create concepts: we must offer alternative concepts to replace those that have become exhausted.

Couldn't one, for example, agree with Kohn that all of life is intertwined in relations of interpretive habit-formation—dispositions—that constitute an *us* beyond the human without calling this thinking? Could we instead call it attunement? For in doing so, we open a path toward an ethics of the world that goes beyond the human without the need for Bennett's "careful course of anthropomorphization," which seems to rely on the reader to simply accept—as a good posthumanist believer—that a concept such as thinking just means something else now. To be sure, some humanists—phenomenologists among them—would argue that only humans are capable of attuned responsivity. The argument of this chapter is that it is precisely this anthropocentric conceit coupled with the posthumanist tendency to continue to "anthropomorphize nature," despite many of their best intentions, that limits our capacity to imagine an ethics beyond the human.

Cynthia Willett, for example, has convincingly shown how attunement and similar concepts allow us to begin to imagine such an ethics, one she refers to as an interspecies ethics. Willett argues that such an ethics has what she calls four layers: 1) subjectless sociality; 2) attunement; 3) the biosocial network as a livable place or home; and 4) animal spirituality and compassion.[29] Already with this simple list, the relational nature of this ethics is evident. For each "layer" can be understood

---

29. Willett 2014: 135.

as an aspect of a relational ontology of existence, within which to exist is above all an indication of an inextricable connection with other such existents. Thus, in contrast to normative ethical theories that expound an "animal ethics" that focuses on the alleviation of animal suffering and re-lies on human-centric capacities such as sympathy or rational principles to do so, Willett's interspecies ethics begins with the necessity of recog-nizing the inextricable intertwining of human and nonhuman animals.

Such an interspecies ethics begins with what she calls subjectless sub-jects. Willett points out that for millennia, the Western metaphysical tradition has excluded from ethics both animals and human infants (one might include women and slaves for a good bit of this time as well) due to their supposed lack of subjectivity or a self. In contrast, she argues that "ethical comportment . . . does not require the presence of a self on either side of the encounter."[30] For it is relationality—and not rational-ity or dignity or will or right or virtue or any other purported human ca-pacity—that is the "ground" of ethics. Indeed, for Willett this relational ethics is most clearly indicated *not* in the more obvious cases of giving, sharing, play, and laughter, but rather in the most basic and carnal social-ity of touch and licking.[31] Relational ethics begins with the responsively attuned touch of bodies; a carnal sociality shared by many animals—hu-man and nonhuman alike.

To the extent that "subjects" and "selves" emerge at all, they do so while attuning. It is not a "self" who attunes—as if mechanically or in-tuitively or rationally—but rather a "self" temporarily emerges as an in-dication of an attunement underway between a plurality of existents. Willett regularly calls this affect attunement, by which subjectless beings "resonate distinctly and dissonantly with one another rather than me-chanically mirror each other."[32] For Willett, "affect attunement is the pri-mary bio-discourse of social creatures."[33] Importantly, such attunement is not only a matter of the face-to-face but also accounts for both solitary and collective ethical responses in various situations as "individuals" and groups attune to what she calls "affect clouds." Throop has articulated this phenomenon with the perhaps clearer name of moral moods.[34] The point in any case is that an interspecies ethics—in fact, an ethics of the

---

30. Willett 2014: 135.
31. Willett 2014: 35. See also Nancy 1997: 59–63; Kearney and Treanor 2015.
32. Willett 2014: 137.
33. Willett 2014: 92.
34. Throop 2014, 2020.

world—begins with the call-and-response of attunement that is indicative of relational existence as such, and not a unique capacity of some being we call human.

It is just this ongoing attunement between and within diverse species—that is to say, inter- and intra-species—that gives way to what Willett calls the biosocial network as a livable place or home. Here it is helpful to recall Nancy's articulation of a world:

> What existence *strives* toward is the world and Being-in-the-world, that is, toward the possibility of making sense. Sense is the reference of all existences between each other ... Existence *desires* to be in the world and to make a world.[35]

Nancy's emphasis on striving and desire is important for thinking Willett's argument. For Willett understands the desire of eros as vital not only to attunement but to what Nancy calls an ethics of the world: "Eros is not a bare striving for pleasure or wild intensity, but a meaning-laden yearning."[36] Rather than meaning, my preference would be to follow Nancy here and say a yearning for the possibility of making sense.

Still, without eros, no ethics.[37] For eros is the desire—the drive—that provides something like an ethical orientation and motivation. Willett is clear: what is missing from many theories of affect is the desire—the drive—that offers orientation and direction, and eros is precisely that missing aspect. As a "drive toward home," Willett wants to emphasize eros as "the drive toward belonging, acknowledgment" and ultimately toward home as a place of freedom.[38] The language here is perhaps a bit too human-centric. Still, the point seems right, and we can make it more appropriately clear by using another nonhuman-centric and relational conceptual register. Thus, we can say that eros is the *drive toward connecting—attuning—with* others, *toward being-with*. This ongoing attunement across and within species—driven and oriented by eros—gives way to a "biosocial network" or world in which we can dwell together in openness. Eros, then, is the orientation and drive toward an ethics of dwelling as an ethics of the world.

---

35. Nancy 2017: 133–34; my italics.
36. Willett 2014: 23.
37. See, for example, Chanter 1995.
38. Willett 2014: 184n66.

Only in situations of attuned dwelling do spirituality and compassion become possible. For only by dwelling-together-well does an openness emerge that allows individuals and groups the "space" to expand the possibilities of their existence. Willett argues, for example, that at least some nonhuman animals may experience forms of spirituality that until now have been reserved solely for humans. Such experiences she describes as moments of "heightened moods or psychic states . . . [that] open up 'oceanic' or holistic experiences of immersion in life and its revitalizing energies."[39] One of the compelling examples she offers of this comes from Barbara Smuts, an anthropologist who works with a troupe of baboons in Gombe National Park in Tanzania. Here is Smuts's description of one such experience as she walked with the troupe along their usual path to their sleeping trees:

> Without any signal perceptible to me, each baboon sat at the edge of a pool on one of the many smooth rocks that lined the edges of the stream. They sat alone or in small clusters, completely quiet, gazing at the water. Even the perpetually noisy juveniles fell into silent contemplation. I joined with them. Half an hour later, again with no perceptible signal [to Smuts], they resumed their journey in what felt like an almost sacramental procession.[40]

Astonished by this communal experience of both collective attunement with one another and collective attunement to what we can simply call existence as such, Smuts described it with the Buddhist term *sangha* meaning spiritual community: "I was stunned by this mysterious expression of what I have come to think of as baboon *sangha*."[41] Astonishment is a reasonable response to this example if one considers the sacred and divine limited to human experiences of God or the gods. But when an experience of the sacred and divine are understood as an attunement with existence as such—or put another way, an attention to the transcendence of relationality that constitutes the very being of us all—then we humans likely have much to learn from these baboons and many other nonhuman animals as well.

Social media may be the scourge of humanity but one benefit it has delivered is the widespread availability of video documentation of what

---

39. Willett 2014: 141.
40. Willett 2014: 100–101.
41. Willett 2014: 101.

Willett calls animal compassion. Increasingly, animal researchers are using these videos because they offer opportunities to observe animal interaction and activity they would otherwise likely never observe in person.[42]
Such videos show us examples of, among other things, animal play, co-
operation, and compassion—including compassion across species. Willett describes interspecies compassion as a suspension of "ordinary moral
judgment or social expectation [that] expands the sense of belonging
beyond normal social attachments and identities . . . and calls into question the human versus animal binaries altogether."[43] Examples of this
interspecies compassion abound. For example, the cow that adopted an
orphaned piglet which I recently saw on a social media post; or Willett's
examples of the forgiveness exhibited by young elephants toward humans to "heal a relational breach" after the latter's transgression; or Kuni
the bonobo who helped a starling escape the cage that Kuni likely never
will. These examples suggest that eros-driven attunement does not close
off once and for all the boundaries of being-with. Rather, such attunement is precisely the existential structure by which all beings—human
and nonhuman alike—transcend their most immediate limitations to
connect with others of potentially any kind.

But here is where Willett's provocative book runs against *its* limitation, one, it should be noted, shared with Kohn's work. For while Willett
makes a strong case for an interspecies ethics primarily based upon what
she calls affect attunement, this ethics is limited to animals—both human and nonhuman. And while Kohn may provide the ontological basis
for an expansion beyond animals to include all of life, his provocation
ends precisely there within the confines of life. But what of other forms
of existence? Indeed, what of nonlife? Surely in the midst of a planetary
crisis,[44] we must at least attempt to think an ethics not simply beyond
the human but beyond the animal as well, and indeed, even beyond life.

This is surely one of the conclusions we can draw from Elizabeth
Povinelli's concern that our modes of thought have for too long focused
laser-like on life. "Western ontologies are covert biontologies," Povinelli
tells us. She continues and explains that Western metaphysics has been
for a long time "a measure of all forms of existence by the qualities of
one form of existence," that is, life.[45] As I have argued elsewhere and

---

42. Gill 2022.
43. Willett 2014: 142.
44. On the planetary, see Chakrabarty 2021.
45. Povinelli 2016: 5.

have been pointing to so far in this chapter, this "one form of existence" is even narrower than life in general. For it has largely been the qualities of a certain conception of the human that has been this measure. This is what I call metaphysical humanism. Still, most certainly Povinelli is correct to say that the distinction between life and nonlife is central to the Western ontological tradition, exemplified since the eighteenth century by biopolitical practices and the more recent critical theoretical interrogation of these.

Increasingly, Povinelli argues, this "biontological orientation and distribution of power" is crumbling and "losing its efficacy as a self-evident backdrop to reason."[46] Climate change, perhaps more than any other experience, is making this apparent to many for the first time. Indeed, climate change is disclosing what Povinelli calls geontology (nonlife being) and geontopower (the power of and over nonlife beings). These concepts "are meant to indicate the current phase of thought and practice that define late liberalism—a phase that is simultaneously reconsolidating [the distinction between life and nonlife] and witnessing its unraveling."[47] Importantly, Povinelli emphasizes that these concepts are not new and alternative ontological theorizations. Rather, they emerge as expressions of the modes of practice and analysis of existence of the Karrabing, the collaborative project that has emerged from Povinelli's "long intimate life" with her Australian Aboriginal kin, friends, and colleagues.[48]

---

46. Povinelli 2016: 6.

47. Povinelli 2016: 179.

48. Povinelli has described Karrabing in the following way:

> Karrabing is not a clan, language or nation. It is an Emmiyangel word referring to the moment when the vast saltwater tides that define the coastal region of the northwest territories of what is now known as Australia reach their lowest point and are about to turn to shore. It is a group of mutually aiding kin, most of whose countries lie along the coastal region of Anson Bay, Northern Territory. It is a concept, aspiration, and endeavor to mobilize film, song, and art as a means of maintaining Indigenous worlds by blocking the extractive powers of late liberalism and its political, social, and economic dimensions and keeping open a space for an otherwise in the current configuration of settler power. The Karrabing is the model of my understanding of a social project. (Povinelli 2021: xi; see also Povinelli 2016: 23)

How can we understand this relationality better in terms of a possible ethics of the world? Povinelli offers a possible starting point with what she calls the "four principles" of a Karrabing analytic of existence. They are:

1. *Things exist through an effort of mutual attention.* This effort is not in the mind but in the activity of endurance.
2. Things are neither born nor die, though they can *turn away from each other and change states.*
3. *In turning away from each other, entities withdraw care for each other.* Thus, the earth is not dying. But the earth may be turning away from certain forms of existence. In this way of thinking the Desert [one of the three figures of geontology that Povinelli articulates along with the Animist and the Virus] is not that in which life does not exist. *A Desert is where a series of entities have withdrawn care for the kinds of entities humans are and thus has made humans into another form of existence*: bone, mummy ash, soil.
4. *We must de-dramatize human life as we squarely take responsibility for what we are doing.* This simultaneous de-dramatization and responsibilization may allow for opening new questions. Rather than Life and Nonlife, we will ask what formations we are keeping in existence or extinguishing.[49]

These four principles articulate well—and particularly those aspects that I have italicized—how I am here trying to think together relational ontology and relational ethics beyond the human. Povinelli is not the only theorist who thinks the relationality of nonlife as a possible starting point for thinking ethically. Similar to Povinelli's focus on such forms of nonlife as rock formations, a creek, fog, and fossils, Oele considers the relationality of soil as offering the possibility for thinking ethics relationally and, ultimately, for creating a much broader community of "us."[50] In particular, Oele focuses on soil pores, which are the interstitial spaces between the solid material soil that constitute about half the total volume of any given amount of soil. Thus, for example, a handful of soil is in fact approximately fifty percent pores, that is, interstitial nonsolid space.[51] As in-between spaces, these pores connect not only the material parts of

---

49. Povinelli 2016: 28; my italics.
50. Oele 2020: chapter 5.
51. Oele 2020: 151, 223.

soil with one another, but also connect these latter with other forms of existence. For example, air and water circulate in pores, and plant roots find space within pores to settle and grow. It would seem, then, that if we hope to respond to the question of how it is between us—and to do so in a manner that extends beyond the human—then we very well ought to attend to that form of existence known as soil pores. For the risk of not doing so, according to Povinelli's analytic, might just be that soil turns its back to us and withdraws care. Put in Povinelli's terms, soil may become Desert. As the in-between space that makes way for and cares for plant roots, we take great risk in not attending to soil pores.

For those readers who may skeptically dismiss much of what they have read in this chapter as little more than the "belief system" or "culture" of some Indigenous peoples and the "weird" thought of some "postmodern" theorists, perhaps the words of Carlo Rovelli, one of the world's most respected physicists, will bring them round. As one of the founding theorists of relational quantum mechanics, Rovelli claims that "what we call 'reality,' is the vast web of interacting entities, of which we are a part, that manifest themselves by interacting with each other." Rovelli continues: "quantum physics demonstrates that the interaction is an inseparable part of phenomena. The unambiguous description of any phenomenon requires the inclusion of all the objects involved in the interaction in which the phenomenon manifests itself."[52] This is precisely what I have been showing throughout this book, what anthropologists and phenomenologists have been saying for at least a century. That is, that all forms of existence only exist as such in relation.

This is the case even for stones, which only becomes obvious when considered from the appropriate temporal scale. For thinking in terms of differential temporalities is key to making sense of the relationality, attendance, and care, that is, the attunement of nonlife. Here is where the work of a physicist helpfully contributes. As Rovelli puts it to an interviewer:

> A stone is just a common flickering of electrons and things and stuff, which remains together—not even forever, of course, because it goes into powder for a long time, for a while. So to better understand the world, I think, we shouldn't reduce it to things. We should reduce it to happenings; and the happenings are always between different systems, always relations . . . We live 100 years, but suppose we

---

52.   Rovelli 2021: 76, 140. See also: Rovelli 2017; Laudisa and Rovelli 2021.

lived a billion years. A stone would be just a moment in which some sand gets together and then it disaggregates, so it's just a momentary getting-together of sand. The permanence of things is—it's a matter of the—we look at them for a short time, with respect to their own staying-together.[53]

Recognizing the differential temporalities of various modes of existence, then, is necessary for a relational ethics of the world. The temporality of stones could be billions of years according to Rovelli, the temporality of soil is many hundreds to thousands of years according to Oele.[54] Only by taking account of the differentiated temporalities between various existents can we begin to understand how different entities are responsive and attend to one another, and in doing so attune and care or turn and withdraw.[55]

Consider, for example, climate change as both an ontological and ethical response to human activity. For decades—if not centuries—humans have—to invoke some of Povinelli's principles listed above—acted *without responsibility and attention* to our relationally intertwined mode of existence with climate, upon which our very being depends. Because the temporality of climate unfolds differently from that of, for example, everyday face-to-face human interaction, only recently are we experiencing the very real possibility that climate is *turning away from and withdrawing its care for us*. In doing so, both climate and human existence is *changing*, and that change experienced by humans is in many cases what we typically call dying, which is just a bio-biased way of articulating a change from life to nonlife.

This is another way of describing what happens when the attunement of relationality breaks down and the various existents—in this case the two complex existents typically named human and climate—turn away from and withdraw mutual care. These two existents unfold with differential temporalities. Humans, for example, exist across multiple temporalities of various duration—a singular lifetime or across generations, for example—though increasingly within the condition of digital-consumer-capitalism the Right Now has come to dominate. Climate,

---

53. Rovelli 2017.
54. Oele 2020: 154.
55. Dipesh Chakrabarty makes similar arguments concerning the necessity of learning to think differential temporalities. See Chakrabarty 2021: 7, 29, 49, 56.

on the other hand, unfolds over a longer duration, typically understood in thirty-year intervals—though significantly observable change, until recently, tended to take place over much longer temporal spans.[56]

Consequently, the onto-ethical relationality between humans and climate may not be as immediately self-evident as, for example, that between two humans standing face-to-face. And yet, once we understand and conceive of attunement across differential temporalities—from the moment-to-moment of the face-to-face, to the decades and centuries of the human-climate intertwining, to the centuries-to-millennia unfolding of life-nonlife relationality—then we can begin to conceive an ethics beyond the human in terms of this relationally ontological structure of existence.

Because attunement happens at differential temporalities relative to different entities, so too dispositions of existence develop differentially depending upon the temporal unfolding of attunement. Humans, for example, attain, develop, and alter their dispositional ways of being-with one another much quicker than rocks or climate attain, develop, and alter their dispositional ways of being-with. Given this temporal differentiation, how do dispositions develop and alter over time? According to Kohn, this occurs as a response to "a disruption of our habituated expectations of what the world is like." For Kohn, of course, this pertains only to life since, as he puts it, the habits of inanimate matter—or nonlife— "have become fixed so as to lose the powers of forming them and losing them."[57] Along with Povinelli, I challenge this bias of life over nonlife.

Still, Kohn is onto something when he highlights the centrality of disruption to the development and alteration of habits or dispositions. As he describes it:

> it is in such moments of "shock" that the habits of the world make themselves manifest. That is, we don't usually notice the habits we inhabit. It is only when the world's habits clash with our expectations that the world in its otherness, and its existent actuality as something other than what we currently are, is revealed. The challenge that follows this disruption is to grow. The challenge is to create a new habit that will encompass this foreign habit and, in the process, to remake ourselves, however momentarily, anew, as one with the world around us . . . it is this very disruption, the *breakdown* of old habits and the

---

56. World Meteorological Organization 2021.
57. Kohn 2013: 63, 62.

rebuilding of new ones, that constitutes our feeling of being alive and in the world. The world is revealed to us, not by the fact that we come to have habits, but in the moments when, forced to abandon our old habits, we come to take up new ones. This is where we can catch glimpses—however mediated—of the emergent real to which we also contribute.[58]

I quote Kohn at length because his emphasis on the disruption and breakdown of habits echoes my concept of moral breakdown.

Recall that in the first two chapters I described the way in which ethics begins with the disruption of the everydayness of dispositional moral life by means of a moral breakdown, and that new embodied dispositions—new relational attunements with our world and its various existents—emerge from this. Moral breakdown occurs when a dissonance arises between a dispositional normativity and its founding exclusion, thus forcing one to reflect on and alter one's already acquired way of being in the world. The consequence is that embodied moral dispositions are "shaped and reshaped," as I put it in my original "Moral Breakdown" article,[59] as we attune with our world and the various entities—humans being just one—with whom we share the world. In this sense, what traditional ethical theory might call "good" is simply an after-the-fact assessment of having reshaped an embodied moral disposition such that the breakdown ends, and one is able once again to dwell in the world.

Kohn makes the strong claim that morality only "emerges within—not beyond—the human," and that conceiving it otherwise is a form of anthropocentric narcissism.[60] This is, of course, absolutely correct if morality (and ethics) is only thought in traditional terms such as the good and the right—or as Kohn interestingly puts it, "privilege[ing] equality," which is not, as far as I know, characteristic of any predominant ethical theory. Still, when traditional ethical theories such as deontology project conceptions of rights or dignity onto "nature," we can most certainly agree with Kohn that this is undoubtedly a form of anthropocentric narcissism.

Kohn seems to limit morality/ethics to the human because he conceives of these as necessitating symbolic reference: the moral is

---

58. Kohn 2013: 63–66; my italics.
59. Zigon 2007: 148.
60. Kohn 2013: 19.

"distinctively human, because to think morally and to act ethically requires symbolic reference." And as he tells us throughout his book: "symbolic reference is distinctively human."[61] To be sure, this is how the human is understood within semiotics, neo-Kantianism, and those modes of thinking that have arisen from these—indeed, much of anthropological thought has. But this is most certainly not the case from within a broadly post-Heideggerian philosophical and theoretical framework, which I would argue has become dominant across most of the (social) humanities today.[62] It is certainly not how I have been articulating the human throughout the chapters of this book.

Let's be clear though: of course, the human has symbolic capacities. But to define the human *as* symbolic is characteristic of a philosophical anthropology that for many today is no longer compelling or convincing. Rather, when the human is instead conceived as relational, situated, and affectively intertwined—as it often is in contemporary social and political theory—then the symbolic becomes less central to how this kind of being is with others—of all kinds—in their shared worlds.

Similarly, when morality is conceived dispositionally, and ethics is conceived in terms of responding to the moral breakdown that occurs as embodied dispositions are disrupted—and this happens through various modalities of attunement that unfold at differential temporalities—then thinking morality and ethics beyond the human is no longer a matter of anthropocentric narcissism but, in fact, necessary. For when conceived as such, we can begin to think an ethics of the world that is adequate to the nonsymbolic relational intertwining of all life and nonlife in the unfolding of existence. Only then can we hear the question of how it is between us appropriately. For only then will the "us" emerge from the between that expands beyond the human to the multitude of other entities with which we must learn to dwell.

Dwelling-together-well is, after all, the telos of ethics. Put another way, dwelling is the ethical imperative of existence. For to dwell is not to be located or emplaced—though it only becomes possible situationally. Rather, dwelling is an existential modality. As dwelling, one is intimately

---

61. Kohn 2013: 133, and, for example, 8 and 57.
62. Note that I am not saying that Heidegger's work has become dominant but rather that Heidegger's work initiated a shift in thinking such that conceiving of the human solely in terms of the symbolic or representation is largely no longer tenable.

intertwined with and concerned for one's world and all its other exist-ents, and one is compelled to maintain the openness of that world in its ongoing attunement with itself. To dwell, then, is at one and the same time to be in a world in such a way that one's being is never pre-limited within a pre-assumed totality and to never pre-limit an other's being. In so doing, dwelling ensures that possibilities for becoming otherwise remain open for both oneself and all others.[63] The political correlate of this ethical imperative of existence, therefore, is to build and maintain worlds in which we can *all* dwell.

Some Closing Words

Have we gone too far? In our attempt to think ethics beyond the hu-man have we stretched a concept beyond recognition? Is this still ethics? Likely, many will say no. Some might agree with Kohn that I am guilty of anthropocentric narcissism. However, recall that the etymological root of ethics (*ēthos*) indicates dwelling in the "abiding sense of the ac-customed place where the living (animals, plants, or otherwise) find their haunt or abode."[64] I would add to this *ēthos* the nonliving as well. Perhaps limiting ethical dwelling to the human is an anthropocentric conceit we can no longer hold to. For surely when we ask today, "how is it between us?" the between about which we ask most certainly extends beyond the human. If we continue to exclude those radically others—those nonhu-man others—from counting as responsive and attuning existents, then I fear that dwelling in the between will continue to become impossible as we remain on our current apocalyptic trajectory.

Perhaps, then, our first response to the despair with which I opened this chapter is—as Chakrabarty has argued[65]—the conceptual creation of a new philosophical anthropology that understands the human as al-ways already relationally intertwined—temporally, materially, ontologi-cally, and, thus, ethically and politically—with all other existents. Put in another register, surely today many have come to recognize that we need what Michel Serres has called a natural contract that recognizes the hermeneutic symbiosis—the attuning intertwinement—of all existents,

---

63. Zigon 2018: 120–21; 2014b. See also: Ingold 2011: 173; Kelly 2019.
64. Baracchi 2008: 53. See also: Heidegger 2011a; Nancy 2002.
65. Chakrabarty 2021: 90–91.

the fragility of which, Serres emphasizes, demands a new ethics.[66] I have been trying to think the structure of this new philosophical anthropology and its more capacious relational ethics throughout this book and particularly so in this chapter.

For let us be honest: none of the traditional ethical theories (and their foundational ontologies) of the so-called Western tradition have fared very well in terms of an ethics of the world. Virtuous men, for example, have not prevented wars. In fact, one might ask: how many wars were started and waged by such men in the very name of upholding, exhibiting, or avenging some virtue or another, or protecting the city or state that is supposedly the seat of virtue? Similarly, consequentialist calculators, for example, did not prevent the global spread of imperialism or capitalism, and indeed many calculated that their spread would bring about the greatest good for the greatest number. Clearly, many peoples around the globe were left out of this count of the greatest number to whom the good pertained. Not to mention that at least one consequence seemingly not calculated was the environmental and planetary degradation that ensued. And lastly, deontological duty followers, for example, did not prevent the Holocaust, but rather at least one of them—Eichmann—found a moral basis for his part in it within Kantian moral philosophy. So, what is it precisely that we expect from these traditional ethical theories to help guide us out of our current planetary and existential crisis? The historical record—if not the theoretical arguments themselves—I believe suggest that we can expect nothing from them at all.

Surely the philosopher Rasmus Dyring is correct when he writes that the "future of 'us'" necessitates "ethical thinking to reckon with its tendency to found itself upon an exclusive, but ontologically unsettled, distinction between the human and the animal."[67] Indeed, I have been arguing that we must go further and demand, following Povinelli, that we transcend the distinction between life and nonlife in our ethical and ontological thinking as well. This is precisely what a relational ontology and ethics offer us. Fear not: this is not a leveling of all existence such that a human and a stone are rendered ontologically and ethically indistinguishable from one another. Far from it. For it is precisely in the "how" of "how is it between us?" that the relational distinctions of existence express themselves as singular beings that differentially unfold—human

---

66. Serres 2011: 37–38; on the hermeneutic nature of the natural contract see pp. 108 and 123; for the need of a new ethics see p. 78.
67. Dyring 2021: 320.

and nonhuman alike. Put another way, it may be relations all the way down, but *how* those relations intertwine and express themselves over time (perhaps vast quantities of time) makes all the difference. Any future ethics worth considering must acknowledge and account for this.

How is it between us? Not great. Conversation has given way to shouting; listening and responding have given way to projection and thematizing the other as fascist, liberal, racist, or snowflake. The between is increasingly characterized by "war" rather than attuned care. How is it between us? Getting worse. Climate change and technology are making it clear that perhaps the "us" narrows too much the question of ethics. If in 1958 Hannah Arendt could limit the between to the human condition, in the twenty-first century that is no longer possible. Today, it has become abundantly clear that the between pertains to the existential condition. The between can no longer be limited to between you and me but must be the between of existence.

And yet, despite the posthuman desires and fantasies regularly expressed today, the way the human responds to the call of this existential between will be decisive. For it is not the human as such that must be left behind, but rather the human tendency to project their own prescriptions, principles, and criteria onto others—all others, human and nonhuman alike. In contrast to this tendency, the relational ethics offered in these chapters argue that above all what is needed today is an ethics of situational attunement that gives way to dwelling. This is an ethical theory that embraces the social and ethnographic fact that ethical practices and relations are ripe with failure. And yet, we must keep going. We must try to attune and dwell again; and then again. This is the risk and uncertainty of ethics. But it is also, I maintain, the hope and promise of ethics. For, if "how is it between us?" is the most fundamental question, then how we respond will be the most fundamental of ethical—as well as political—indeed, the most fundamental of existential replies.

References

Agamben, Giorgio. 2009. *The Coming Community*. Minneapolis: University of Minnesota Press.

———. 2015. *Stasis: Civil War as a Political Paradigm*. Stanford, CA: Stanford University Press.

Alexander, Bruce K. 2008. *The Globalization of Addiction: A Study in Poverty of the Spirit*. Oxford: Oxford University Press.

Alexander, Michelle. 2012. *The New Jim Crow: Mass Incarceration in the Age of Colorblindness*. New York: New Press.

Amrute, Sareeta. 2019. "Of Techno-Ethics and Techno-Affects." *Feminist Review* 123 (1): 56–73.

Anderson, Benedict. 1999. *Imagined Communities: Reflections on the Origin and Spread of Nationalism*. Revised edition. London: Verso.

Arendt, Hannah. 1973. *The Origins of Totalitarianism*. New York: Harcourt, Brace, Jovanovich.

———. 1978. *The Life of the Mind*. New York: Harcourt.

———. 1998. *The Human Condition*. Chicago: University of Chicago Press.

———. 2005. "Introduction into Politics." In *The Promise of Politics*. New York: Schocken Books.

———. 2006. *Eichmann in Jerusalem: A Report on the Banality of Evil*. New York: Penguin Books.

———. 2018. *Thinking Without a Banister: Essays in Understanding, 1953–1975*. Edited by Jerome Kohn. New York: Schocken Books.

Asad, Talal. 1986. "The Concept of Cultural Translation in British Social Anthropology." In *Writing Culture: The Poetics and Politics of Ethnography*, edited by James Clifford and George E. Marcus, 141–64. Berkeley: University of California Press.

———. 1993. *Genealogies of Religion: Discipline and Reasons of Power in Christianity and Islam*. Baltimore: Johns Hopkins University Press.

———. 2003. *Formations of the Secular: Christianity, Islam, Modernity*. Stanford, CA: Stanford University Press.

Aulino, Felicity. 2019. *Rituals of Care: Karmic Politics in an Aging Thailand*. Ithaca, NY: Cornell University Press.

Babich, Babette. 2015. "Nietzsche and the Ubiquity of Hermeneutics." In *The Routledge Companion to Hermeneutics*, edited by Jeff Malpas and Hans-Helmuth Gander, 83–97. London and New York: Routledge.

Baracchi, Claudia. 2008. *Aristotle's Ethics as First Philosophy*. Cambridge: Cambridge University Press.

Barad, Karen Michelle. 2007. *Meeting the Universe Halfway: Quantum Physics and the Entanglement of Matter and Meaning*. Durham, NC: Duke University Press.

Bauman, Zygmunt. 2001. *Community: Seeking Safety in an Insecure World*. Cambridge: Polity Press.

Beiner, Ronald. 1982. "Hannah Arendt on Judging." In *Hannah Arendt: Lectures on Kant's Political Philosophy*, edited by Ronald Beiner, 89–156. Chicago: University of Chicago Press.

Benjamin, Ruha. 2019. *Race After Technology: Abolitionist Tools for the New Jim Code*. Cambridge: Polity Press.

Bennett, Jane. 2010. *Vibrant Matter: A Political Ecology of Things*. Durham, NC: Duke University Press.

Berardi, Franco "Bifo." 2016. "The Coming Global Civil War: Is There Any Way Out?" *E-Flux* #69 (January 2016). https://www.e-flux.com/journal/69/60582/the-coming-global-civil-war-is-there-any-way-out/.

Bialecki, Jon. 2017. *A Diagram for Fire: Miracles and Variations in an American Charismatic Movement*. Oakland: University of California Press.

Blanchot, Maurice. 1988. *The Unavowable Community*. Barrytown, NY: Station Hill Press.

Bourgois, Philippe. 2000. "Disciplining Addictions: The Bio-Politics of Methadone and Heroin in the United States." *Culture, Medicine and Psychiatry* 24: 165–95.

Braver, Lee. 2014. *Groundless Grounds: A Study of Wittgenstein and Heidegger.* Cambridge, MA: MIT Press.

Brown, Charles S., and Ted Toadvine, eds. 2003. *Eco-Phenomenology: Back to the Earth Itself.* Albany: State University of New York Press.

Brown, Peter. 1989. *The World of Late Antiquity.* New York: W. W. Norton & Company.

Browning, Christopher R. 1998. *Ordinary Men: Reserve Police Battalion 101 and the Final Solution in Poland.* New York: Harper Perennial.

Bubandt, Nils, and Thomas Schwarz Wentzer, eds. 2023. *Philosophy on Fieldwork: Case Studies in Anthropological Analysis.* London and New York: Routledge.

Butler, Judith. 2005. *Giving an Account of Oneself.* New York: Fordham University Press.

Caputo, John D. 1987. *Radical Hermeneutics: Repetition, Deconstruction, and the Hermeneutic Project.* Bloomington: Indiana University Press.

———. 1997. *Deconstruction in a Nutshell: A Conversation with Jacques Derrida.* New York: Fordham University Press.

———. 2018. *Hermeneutics: Facts and Interpretation in the Age of Information.* New York: Pelican Books.

Chakrabarty, Dipesh. 2015. "Moods of the Anthropocene: Interview with Dipesh Chakrabarty (by Liesbeth Koot)." In *The Geologic Imagination*, edited by Arie Altena, Mirna Belina, and Lucas van der Velden, 93–104. Amsterdam: Sonic Acts Press.

———. 2021. *The Climate of History in a Planetary Age.* Chicago: University of Chicago Press.

Chanter, Tina. 1995. *Ethics of Eros: Irigaray's Rewriting of the Philosophers.* New York: Routledge.

Cheney-Lippold, John. 2017. *We Are Data: Algorithms and the Making of Our Digital Selves.* New York: New York University Press.

Clingerman, Forrest, Brian Treanor, Martin Drenthen, and David Utsler, eds. 2014. *Interpreting Nature: The Emerging Field of Environmental Hermeneutics.* New York: Fordham University Press.

Connolly, William E. 2013. *The Fragility of Things: Self-Organizing Processes, Neoliberal Fantasies, and Democratic Activism.* Durham, NC: Duke University Press.

Crapanzano, Vincent. 2004. *Imaginative Horizons: An Essay in Literary-Philosophical Anthropology.* Chicago: University of Chicago Press.

Critchley, Simon. 2007. *Infinitely Demanding: Ethics of Commitment, Politics of Resistance*. London: Verso.

Das, Veena. 2012. "Ordinary Ethics." In *A Companion to Moral Anthropology*, edited by Didier Fassin, 133–49. Malden, MA: Wiley-Blackwell.

———. 2015. "What Does Ordinary Ethics Look Like?" In *Four Lectures on Ethics: Anthropological Perspectives*, 53–125. Chicago: Hau Books.

———. 2020. *Textures of the Ordinary: Doing Anthropology after Wittgenstein*. New York: Fordham University Press.

Daston, Lorraine, and Peter Galison 2010. *Objectivity*. New York: Zone Books.

David, Marian. 2020. "The Correspondence Theory of Truth." In *The Stanford Encyclopedia of Philosophy*. https://plato.stanford.edu/archives/fall2016/entries/truth-correspondence/.

Deleuze, Gilles. 1992. "Postscript on the Societies of Control." *October* 59 (Winter): 3–7.

Derrida, Jacques. 1978. "Violence and Metaphysics: An Essay on the Thought of Emmanuel Levinas." In *Writing and Difference*, 126–27. Chicago: University of Chicago Press.

———. 1992a. "Force of Law: The 'Mystical Foundation of Authority.'" In *Deconstruction and the Possibility of Justice*, edited by Drucilla Cornell, Michel Rosenfeld, and David Gray Carlson, 3–67. New York and London: Routledge.

———. 1992b. *Given Time: 1. Counterfeit Money*. Chicago: University of Chicago Press.

———. 1994. *Specters of Marx: The State of the Debt, the Work of Mourning, and the New International*. New York and London: Routledge.

———. 1997. "The Villanova Roundtable: A Conversation with Jacques Derrida." In *Deconstruction in a Nutshell: A Conversation with Jacques Derrida*, edited by John D. Caputo, 3–28. New York: Fordham University Press.

———. 1999. "Hospitality, Justice and Responsibility: A Dialogue with Jacques Derrida." In *Questioning Ethics: Contemporary Debates in Philosophy*, edited by Richard Kearney and Mark Dooley, 65–83. London: Routledge.

Derrida, Jacques, and Anne Dufourmantelle. 2000. *Of Hospitality*. Stanford, CA: Stanford University Press.

Dilts, Andrew. 2014. *Punishment and Inclusion: Race, Membership, and the Limits of American Liberalism*. New York: Fordham University Press.

Dyring, Rasmus. 2018a. "From Moral Facts to Human Finitude: On the Problem of Freedom in the Anthropology of Ethics." *HAU: Journal of Ethnographic Theory* 8 (1/2): 223–35.

———. 2018b. "The Provocation of Freedom." In *Moral Engines: Exploring the Ethical Drives in Human Life*, edited by Cheryl Mattingly, Rasmus Dyring, Maria Louw, and Thomas Schwarz Wentzer, 116–33. New York and Oxford: Berghahn Books.

———. 2020. "Emplaced at the Thresholds of Life: Toward a Phenomenological an-Archaeology of Borders and Human Bounding." In *Debating and Defining Borders: Philosophical and Theoretical Perspectives*, edited by Anthony Cooper and Soren Tinning, 97–111. London and New York: Routledge.

———. 2021. "The Future of 'Us': A Critical Phenomenology of the Aporias of Ethical Community in the Anthropocene." *Philosophy and Social Criticism* 47 (3): 304–21.

Esposito, Roberto. 2010. *Communitas: The Origin and Destiny of Community*. Stanford, CA: Stanford University Press.

———. 2013. *Communitas: The Origin and Destiny of Community; Terms of the Political: Community, Immunity, Biopolitics*. New York: Fordham University Press.

Faubion, James D. 2011. *An Anthropology of Ethics*. Cambridge: Cambridge University Press.

Finn, Ed. 2017. *What Algorithms Want: Imagination in the Age of Computing*. Cambridge, MA: MIT Press.

Foucault, Michel. 1997. "Polemics, Politics, and Problematizations." In *Ethics: Subjectivity and Truth*, edited by Paul Rabinow, 111–19. New York: The New Press.

Fritsch, Matthias, Philippe Lynes, and David Wood, eds. 2018. *Eco-Deconstruction: Derrida and Environmental Philosophy*. New York: Fordham University Press.

Gadamer, Hans-Georg. 1997. *Truth and Method*. New York: Continuum.

Garcia, Angela. 2010. *The Pastoral Clinic: Addiction and Dispossession along the Rio Grande*. Berkeley: University of California Press.

Gill, Victoria. 2022. "Why Scientists Are Also Watching Animal YouTube Videos." *BBC News*, May 29, 2022. https://www.bbc.com/news/science-environment-61609679.

Goffman, Alice. 2014. *On the Run: Fugitive Life in an American City*. New York: Picador.

Gubser, Michael. 2014. *The Far Reaches: Phenomenology, Ethics, and Social Renewal in Central Europe*. Stanford, CA: Stanford University Press.

Guenther, Lisa. 2006. *The Gift of the Other: Levinas and the Politics of Reproduction*. Albany: State University of New York Press.

Gupta, Akhil, and James Ferguson. 1992. "Beyond 'Culture': Space, Identity, and the Politics of Difference." *Cultural Anthropology* 7 (1): 6–23.

Hadot, Pierre. 1995. *Philosophy as a Way of Life*. Malden, MA: Blackwell Publishing.

Hari, Johann. 2015. *Chasing the Scream: The First and Last Days of the War on Drugs*. London: Bloomsbury Circus.

Havel, Václav. 1992. "The Power of the Powerless." In *Open Letters: Selected Writings 1965–1990*, 125–214. New York: Vintage Books.

Heidegger. Martin. 1968. *What Is Called Thinking?* New York: Harper Colophon Books.

———. 1975a. "Language." In *Poetry, Language, Thought*, 187–210. New York: Harper Colophon Books.

———. 1975b. "The Anaximander Fragment." In *Early Greek Thinking*, 13–58. New York: Harper & Row.

———. 1977. "The Question Concerning Technology." In *The Question Concerning Technology and Other Essays*, 3–35. New York: Harper & Row.

———. 1996. *Being and Time*. Translated by Joan Stambaugh. Albany: SUNY Press.

———. 2011a. "Letter on Humanism." In *Basic Writings*, edited by David Farrell Krell, 141–81. London and New York: Routledge.

———. 2011b. "On the Essence of Truth." In *Basic Writings*, edited by David Farrell Krell, 59–82. London and New York: Routledge.

Hemment, Julie. 2015. *Youth Politics in Putin's Russia: Producing Patriots and Entrepreneurs*. Bloomington: Indiana University Press.

Hirschkind, Charles. 2006. *The Ethical Soundscape: Cassette Sermons and Islamic Counterpublics*. New York: Columbia University Press.

Holbraad, Martin. 2012. *Truth in Motion: The Recursive Anthropology of Cuban Divination*. Chicago: University of Chicago Press.

Holbraad, Martin, and Morten Axel Pedersen. 2017. *The Ontological Turn: An Anthropological Exposition*. Cambridge: Cambridge University Press.

Husserl, Edmund. 1962. *Ideas: General Introduction to Pure Phenomenology*. New York: Collier Books.

Ingold, Tim. 2011. *The Perception of the Environment: Essays on Livelihood, Dwelling and Skill*. London: Routledge.

———. 2013. "Prospect." In *Biosocial Becomings: Integrating Social and Biological Anthropology*, edited by Tim Ingold and Gisli Palsson, 1–21. Cambridge: Cambridge University Press.

———. 2017. "On Human Correspondence." *Journal of the Royal Anthropological Institute* 23 (1): 9–27.

James, Ian. 2006. *The Fragmentary Demand: An Introduction to the Philosophy of Jean-Luc Nancy*. Stanford, CA: Stanford University Press.

Keane, Webb. 2015. *Ethical Life: Its Natural and Social Histories*. Princeton, NJ: Princeton University Press.

Kearney, Richard, and Brian Treanor, eds. 2015. *Carnal Hermeneutics*. New York: Fordham University Press.

Kelleher, John D., and Brendan Tierney. 2018. *Data Science*. Cambridge, MA: MIT Press.

Kelly, Elaine. 2019. *Dwelling in the Age of Climate Change: The Ethics of Adaptation*. Edinburgh: Edinburgh University Press.

Kohn, Eduardo. 2013. *How Forests Think: Toward an Anthropology Beyond the Human*. Berkeley: University of California Press.

Laclau, Ernesto, and Chantal Mouffe. 2001. *Hegemony and Socialist Strategy: Towards a Radical Democratic Politics*. London: Verso.

Laidlaw, James. 2002. "For an Anthropology of Ethics and Freedom." *Journal of the Royal Anthropological Institute* 8 (2): 311–32.

———. 2014. *The Subject of Virtue: An Anthropology of Ethics and Freedom*. Cambridge: Cambridge University Press.

Lambek, Michael. 2010a. "Introduction." In *Ordinary Ethics: Anthropology, Language, and Action*, edited by Michael Lambek, 1–36. New York: Fordham University Press.

———. 2010b. "Toward an Ethics of the Act." In *Ordinary Ethics: Anthropology, Language, and Action*, edited by Michael Lambek, 39–63. New York: Fordham University Press.

Laudisa, Federico, and Carlo Rovelli. 2021. "Relational Quantum Mechanics." In *The Stanford Encyclopedia of Philosophy*, edited by Edward N. Zalta. https://plato.stanford.edu/archives/win2021/entries/qm-relational/.

Leistle, Bernhard. 2023. "Waldenfels among Spirits and Saints in Morocco." In *Philosophy on Fieldwork: Case Studies in Anthropological Analysis*, edited by Nils Bubandt and Thomas Schwarz Wentzer, 463–79. London and New York: Routledge.

Lengen, Samuel. 2019. "How Much Is Your Data Worth to Tech Companies? Lawmakers Want to Tell You, but It's Not That Easy to Calculate." *The Conversation*, July 11, 2019. https://theconversation.com/how-much-is-your-data-worth-to-tech-companies-lawmakers-want-to-tell-you-but-its-not-that-easy-to-calculate-119716.

Lester, Rebecca. 2019. *Famished: Eating Disorders and Failed Care in America*. Oakland: University of California Press.

Levinas, Emmanuel. 2011. *Totality and Infinity: An Essay on Exteriority*. Pittsburgh, PA: Duquesne University Press.

Locke, John. 1980. *Second Treatise of Government*. Indianapolis, IN: Hackett Publishing Company.

Løgstrup, Knud Ejler. 1997. *The Ethical Demand*. Notre Dame, IN: University of Notre Dame Press.

MacIntyre, Alasdair. 1981. *After Virtue*. Notre Dame, IN: University of Notre Dame Press.

———. 1988. *Whose Justice? Which Rationality?* Notre Dame, IN: University of Notre Dame Press.

———. 2016. *Ethics in the Conflicts of Modernity: An Essay on Desire, Practical Reasoning, and Narrative*. Cambridge: Cambridge University Press.

Mahmood, Saba. 2005. *Politics of Piety: The Islamic Revival and the Feminist Subject*. Princeton, NJ: Princeton University Press.

Marion, Jean-Luc. 2002. *Being Given: Toward a Phenomenology of Givenness*. Stanford, CA: Stanford University Press.

Mattingly, Cheryl. 2012. "Two Virtue Ethics and the Anthropology of Morality." *Anthropological Theory* 12 (2): 161–84.

———. 2014. *Moral Laboratories: Family Peril and the Struggle for a Good Life*. Berkeley: University of California Press.

———. 2018. "Ethics, Immanent Transcendence and the Experimental Narrative Self." In *Moral Engines: Exploring the Ethical Drives in Human Life*, edited by Cheryl Mattingly, Rasmus Dyring, Maria Louw, and Thomas Schwarz Wentzer, 39–60. New York and Oxford: Berghahn Books.

———. 2019. "Defrosting Concepts, Destabilizing Doxa: Critical Phenomenology and the Perplexing Particular." *Anthropological Theory* 19 (4): 415–39.

Mattingly, Cheryl, Rasmus Dyring, Maria Louw, and Thomas Schwarz Wentzer., eds. 2018. *Moral Engines: Exploring the Ethical Drives in Human Life*. New York and Oxford: Berghahn Books.

Mauss, Marcel. 1997. "Gift, Gift." In *The Logic of the Gift: Toward an Ethics of Generosity*, edited by Alan D. Schrift, 28–32. New York: Routledge.

———. 1990. *The Gift*. New York: W. W. Norton, 1990.

Mazzarella, William. 2017. *The Mana of Mass Society*. Chicago: University of Chicago Press.

Mckay, Francis. 2018. "Telic Attunements: Moods and Ultimate Values (Among Meditation Practitioners in the United States)." *Ethos* 46 (4): 498–515.

McLean, Katherine. 2011. "The Biopolitics of Needle Exchange in the United States." *Critical Public Health* 21 (1): 71–79.

McLean, Stuart. 2017. *Fictionalizing Anthropology: Encounters and Fabulations at the Edges of the Human*. Minneapolis: University of Minnesota Press.

Merleau-Ponty, Maurice. 1997. *The Visible and the Invisible*. Evanston, IL: Northwestern University Press.

———. 2012. *Phenomenology of Perception*. London: Routledge.

Mitchell, Andrew J. 2010. "The Fourfold." In *Martin Heidegger: Key Concepts*, edited by Bret W. Davis, 208–18. Durham, UK: Acumen Publishing.

Nancy, Jean-Luc. 1991. *The Inoperative Community*. Minneapolis: University of Minnesota Press.

———. 1993. *The Experience of Freedom*. Stanford, CA: Stanford University Press.

———. 1997. *The Sense of the World*. Minneapolis: University of Minnesota Press.

———. 2000. *Being Singular Plural*. Translated by Robert Richardson and Anne O'Byrne. Stanford CA: Stanford University Press.

———. 2002. "Heidegger's 'Originary Ethics.'" In *Heidegger and Practical Philosophy*, edited by François Raffoul and David Pettigrew, 65–85. Albany: State University of New York Press.

———. 2017. *The Possibility of a World: Conversations with Pierre-Philippe Jandin*. Translated by Travis Holloway and Flor Méchain. New York: Fordham University Press.

Noble, Safiya Umoja. 2018. *Algorithms of Oppression: How Search Engines Reinforce Racism*. New York: New York University Press.

O'Byrne, Anne. 2015. "Umbilicus: Toward a Hermeneutics of Generational Difference." In *Carnal Hermeneutics*, edited by Richard Kearney and Brian Treanor, 182–94. New York: Fordham University Press.

Ochs, Elinor. 2012. "Experiencing Language." *Anthropological Theory* 12 (2): 142–60.

Oele, Marjolein. 2020. *E-Co-Affectivity: Exploring Pathos at Life's Material Interfaces.* Albany: State University of New York Press.

O'Neil, Cathy. 2016. *Weapons of Math Destruction: How Big Data Increases Inequality and Threatens Democracy.* New York: Broadway Books.

Patočka, Jan. 1998. *Body, Community, Language, World.* Chicago: Open Court.

Pentland, Alex. 2009. "Reality Mining of Mobile Communications: Toward a New Deal on Data." *The Global Information Technology Report 2008– 2009*, 75–80. Geneva: World Economic Forum.

Pinto, Sarah. 2014. *Daughters of Parvati: Women and Madness in Contemporary India.* Philadelphia: University of Pennsylvania Press.

Porter, Theodore M. 1995. *Trust in Numbers: The Pursuit of Objectivity in Science and Public Life.* Princeton, NJ: Princeton University Press.

Povinelli, Elizabeth A. 2011. *Economies of Abandonment: Social Belonging and Endurance in Late Liberalism.* Durham, NC: Duke University Press.

———. 2016. *Geontologies: A Requiem to Late Liberalism.* Durham, NC: Duke University Press.

———. 2021. *Between Gaia and Ground: Four Axioms of Existence and the Ancestral Catastrophe of Late Liberalism.* Durham, NC, and London: Duke University Press.

Rapport, Nigel. 2015. "Anthropology through Levinas: Knowing the Uniqueness of Ego and the Mystery of Otherness." *Current Anthropology* 56 (2): 256–76.

———. 2019. "Anthropology through Levinas (Further Reflections): On Humanity, Being, Culture, Violation, Sociality, and Morality." *Current Anthropology* 60 (1): 70–90.

Robbins, Joel. 2004. *Becoming Sinners: Christianity and Moral Torment in a Papua New Guinea Society.* Berkeley: University of California Press.

———. 2007. "Between Reproduction and Freedom: Morality, Value, and Radical Cultural Change." *Ethnos* 72 (3): 293–314.

———. 2009. "Value, Structure, and the Range of Possibilities: A Response to Zigon." *Ethnos* 74 (2): 277–85.

———. 2010. "Recognition, Reciprocity, and Justice: Melanesian Reflections on the Rights of Relationships." In *Mirrors of Justice: Law and Power in the Post-Cold War Era*, edited by Kamari Maxine Clarke and Mark Goodale, 171–90. Cambridge: Cambridge University Press.

———. 2016. "What Is the Matter with Transcendence? On the Place of Religion in the New Anthropology of Ethics." *Journal of the Royal Anthropological Institute* 22 (4): 767–81.

———. 2020. *Theology and the Anthropology of Christian Life*. Oxford: Oxford University Press.

Roe, Gordon. 2005. "Harm Reduction as Paradigm: Is Better than Bad Good Enough? The Origins of Harm Reduction." *Critical Public Health* 15 (3): 243–50.

Rorty, Richard. 1979. *Philosophy and the Mirror of Nature*. Princeton, NJ: Princeton University Press.

Rovelli, Carlo. 2017. "All Reality is Interaction." On Being with Krista Tippett (podcast), March 16, 2017. https://onbeing.org/programs/carlo-rovelli-all-reality-is-interaction/#audio.

———. 2021. *Helgoland: Making Sense of the Quantum Revolution*. New York: Riverhead Books.

Sahlins, Marshall. 1972. *Stone Age Economics*. Chicago: Aldine Atherton.

———. 2011a. "What Kinship Is (Part One)." *Journal of the Royal Anthropological Institute* 17 (1): 2–19.

———. 2011b. "What Kinship Is (Part Two)." *Journal of the Royal Anthropological Institute* 17 (2): 227–42.

Samuels, Annemarie. 2019. *After the Tsunami: Disaster Narratives and the Remaking of Everyday Life in Aceh*. Honolulu: University of Hawaii Press.

Sartre, Jean-Paul. 1968. *Communists and the Peace*. New York: George Braziller.

Scherz, China. 2014. *Having People, Having Heart: Charity, Sustainable Development, and Problems of Dependence in Central Uganda*. Chicago: University of Chicago Press.

Scherz, Paul. 2019. *Science and Christian Ethics*. Cambridge: Cambridge University Press.

———. 2022. *Tomorrow's Troubles: Risk, Anxiety, and Prudence in an Age of Algorithmic Governance*. Washington, DC: Georgetown University Press.

Scranton, Roy. 2015. *Learning to Die in the Anthropocene: Reflections on the End of a Civilization*. San Francisco: City Lights Books.

Seale-Feldman, Aidan. 2020. "The Work of Disaster: Building Back Otherwise in Post-Earthquake Nepal." *Cultural Anthropology* 35 (2): 237–63.

Serres, Michel. 2011. *The Natural Contract*. Ann Arbor: University of Michigan Press.

Shohet, Merav. 2021. *Silence and Sacrifice: Family Stories of Care and the Limits of Love in Vietnam*. Oakland: University of California Press.

Sorgen, Jeremy. 2021. "Pragmatic Ethics: Rethinking Environmental Practice and Social Change." PhD dissertation, University of Virginia.

Srnicek, Nick, and Alex Williams. 2015. *Inventing the Future: Postcapitalism and a World Without Work*. London: Verso.

Stasch, Rupert. 2009. *Society of Others: Kinship and Mourning in a West Papuan Place*. Berkeley: University of California Press.

Stevenson, Bryan. 2011. "Drug Policy, Criminal Justice and Mass Imprisonment." Working paper prepared for the First Meeting of the Global Commission on Drug Policies, January 24–25, 2011. Geneva.

Stewart, Kathleen. 2007. *Ordinary Affects*. Durham, NC: Duke University Press.

Strathern, Marilyn. 1988. *The Gender of the Gift*. Berkeley: University of California Press.

———. 2020. *Relations: An Anthropological Account*. Durham, NC: Duke University Press.

Throop, C. Jason. 2008. "On the Problem of Empathy: The Case of Yap, Federated States of Micronesia." *Ethos* 36 (4): 402–26.

———. 2010a. *Suffering and Sentiment: Exploring the Vicissitudes of Experience and Pain in Yap*. Berkeley: University of California Press.

———. 2010b. "Latitudes of Loss: On the Vicissitudes of Empathy." *American Ethnologist* 37 (4): 771–82.

———. 2014. "Moral Moods." *Ethos* 42 (1): 65–83.

———. 2018. "Being Otherwise: On Regret, Morality, and Mood." In *Moral Engines: Exploring the Ethical Drives in Human Life*, edited by Cheryl Mattingly, Rasmus Dyring, Maria Louw, and Thomas Schwarz Wentzer, 61–82. New York and Oxford: Berghahn Books.

———. 2020. "Meteorological Moods and Atmospheric Attunements." In *Vulnerability and the Politics of Care*, edited by Victoria Browne, Doerthe Rosenow, and Jason Danely, 60–77. Proceedings of the British Academy Publication 235. Oxford: Oxford University Press.

———. "Looming." *Puncta: Journal of Critical Phenomenology* 5 (22): 67–86.

Tidey, Sylvia. 2022. *Ethics or the Right Thing? Corruption and Care in the Age of Good Governance*. Chicago: Hau Books.

Toadvine, Ted. 2009. *Merleau-Ponty's Philosophy of Nature*. Evanston, IL: Northwestern University Press.

Trigg, Dylan. 2014. "Bodily Moods and Unhomely Environments: The Hermeneutics of Agoraphobia and the Spirit of Place." In *Interpreting Nature: The Emerging Field of Environmental Hermeneutics*, edited by Forrest Clingerman, Brian Treanor, Martin Drenthen and David Utsler, 160–77. New York: Fordham University Press.

UNDOC. 2014. "World Drug Report 2014." New York: United Nations Office on Drugs and Crime.

Varma, Saiba. 2020. *The Occupied Clinic: Militarism and Care in Kashmir*. Durham, NC: Duke University Press.

Villa, Dana R. 1999. *Politics, Philosophy, Terror: Essays on the Thought of Hannah Arendt*. Princeton, NJ: Princeton University Press.

Wagner, Roy. 2001. *The Anthropology of the Subject: Holographic Worldview in New Guinea and Its Meaning and Significance for the World of Anthropology*. Berkeley: University of California Press.

Waldenfels, Bernhard. 2011. *Phenomenology of the Alien: Basic Concepts*. Evanston, IL: Northwestern University Press.

Watts, Edward J. 2015. *The Final Pagan Generation: Rome's Unexpected Path to Christianity*. Oakland: University of California Press.

Wentzer, Thomas Schwarz. 2018a. "Human, the Responding Being: Considerations Towards a Philosophical Anthropology of Responsiveness." In *Moral Engines: Exploring the Ethical Drives in Human Life*, edited by Cheryl Mattingly, Rasmus Dyring, Maria Louw, and Thomas Schwarz Wentzer, 211–29. New York and Oxford: Berghahn Books.

———. 2018b. "Selma's Response: A Case for Responsive Anthropology." *Hau: Journal of Ethnographic Theory* 8 (1/2): 211–22.

Wickham, Chris. 2016. *Medieval Europe*. New Haven, CT: Yale University Press.

Willett, Cynthia. 2014. *Interspecies Ethics*. 2014. New York: Columbia University Press.

Wolin, Sheldon. 2004. *Politics and Vision*. Expanded edition. Princeton, NJ: Princeton University Press.

World Meteorological Organization. 2021. "Climate." https://public.wmo.int/en/our-mandate/climate.

Wright, Fiona. 2018. *The Israeli Radical Left: An Ethics of Complicity*. Philadelphia: University of Pennsylvania Press.

Young, Iris Marion. 1990. *Justice and the Politics of Difference*. Princeton, NJ: Princeton University Press.

Yurchak, Alexei. 2006. *Everything Was Forever, Until It Was No More: The Last Soviet Generation*. Princeton, NJ: Princeton University Press.

Zigon, Jarrett. 2007. "Moral Breakdown and the Ethical Demand: A Theoretical Framework for an Anthropology of Moralities." *Anthropological Theory* 7 (2): 131–50.

———. 2008. *Morality: An Anthropological Perspective*. Oxford: Berg Publishers.

———. 2009a. "Within a Range of Possibilities: Morality and Ethics in Social Life." *Ethnos* 74 (2): 251–76.

———. 2009b. "Phenomenological Anthropology and Morality: A Reply to Robbins." *Ethnos* 74 (2): 286–88.

———. 2010. *Making the New Post-Soviet Person: Moral Experience in Contemporary Moscow*. Leiden: Brill.

———. 2011. *HIV Is God's Blessing: Rehabilitating Morality in Neoliberal Russia*. Berkeley: University of California Press.

———. 2012. "Narratives." In *A Companion to Moral Anthropology*, edited by Didier Fassin, 204–20. Malden, MA: Wiley-Blackwell.

———. 2014a. "Attunement and Fidelity: Two Ontological Conditions for Morally Being-in-the-World." *Ethos* 42 (1): 16–30.

———. 2014b. "An Ethics of Dwelling and a Politics of World-Building: A Critical Response to Ordinary Ethics." *Journal of the Royal Anthropological Institute*, n.s., 20 (4): 746–64.

———. 2015. "What Is a Situation?: An Assemblic Ethnography of the Drug War." *Cultural Anthropology* 30 (3): 501–24.

———. 2018. *Disappointment: Toward a Critical Hermeneutics of Worldbuilding*. New York: Fordham University Press.

———. 2019. *A War on People: Drug User Politics and a New Ethics of Community*. Oakland: University of California Press.

Zigon, Jarrett, and C. Jason Throop. 2014. "Moral Experience: Introduction." *Ethos* 42 (1): 1–15.

Zuboff, Shoshana. 2019. *The Age of Surveillance Capitalism: The Fight for a Human Future at the New Frontier of Power*. New York: PublicAffairs.